ANTHOLOGY OF GERMAN POETRY

Through the 19th Century

*In English Translations with
the German Originals*

Edited by
ALEXANDER GODE
and
FREDERICK UNGAR

FREDERICK UNGAR PUBLISHING CO.
NEW YORK

THIS VOLUME WAS PREPARED WITH THE
EDITORIAL COLLABORATION OF THE
AMERICAN TRANSLATORS ASSOCIATION

FOREWORD

'Indeed every translator
is a prophet to his people!'
—*Goethe*

Much has been said, and justly, about the peculiar difficulties of translating poetry. It has even been claimed that any such attempt is doomed to failure. No one can indeed deny that transposing a poem into another language entails the inevitable sacrifice of at least some of its poetic value. Only for very short spans, and this only because of a happy coincidence between two languages in meaning, meter, mood, and diction – something that never happens over long stretches – is the 'absolute' translation achieved.

But should a full acknowledgment of the perils lying in wait for the translator lead to a resigned conclusion that not even an attempt should be made to translate poetry? Is man in all his pursuits, especially in the arts, so committed to the absolute that nothing less is worthy of his endeavors? Or is not rather the opposite true—that acquiescence in the attainable and not the achievement of the absolute is the law of life, and that perfection is no more than a beacon toward which our efforts are directed?

All this, of course, is self-evident; yet it may be well to say it clearly in rebutting the lofty statements so often uttered by poetry's high priests, that if we cannot have perfection we would rather have nothing at all.

There have been many real achievements in translation of poetry, congenial translations that are works of art in their own right; these have often been the triumphs of poets of the first rank who, through the centuries, have been attracted by the challenge of rendering foreign poetry into their mother tongue. This challenge only sharpens what is usually a spontaneous and irresistible desire to make a treasured poem accessible to the many who would surely appreciate it as much, if only they knew it. Those who have undertaken this task – this magnificently exacting task – deserve well of us. They are indeed 'prophets to their people'.

A few words about the unusual genesis of this anthology: This project, undertaken with the editorial collaboration of the American Translators Association, was launched in the conviction that a substantial amount of unpublished translations from the German must surely exist and that lovers of German poetry might be more than willing to attempt new translations for a collection intended to promote the appreciation of German poetry. Invitations went out to professional translators in the English-speaking world, and to members of the teaching profession, to come forth with their personal treasures, or to make this the occasion to complete a long considered translation, or to nominate a favorite version that was the work of someone else.

The response to this invitation was lively beyond expectations; the active interest evidenced by wide participation was highly gratifying.

The great freedom granted the contributors to this anthology in selecting the individual poems to be translated, with only a minimum of direction by the editors, will explain why this collection is not as well rounded as it might otherwise have been. It seemed important to restrict the contributors' own choices as little as possible so as to insure that they would undertake the translation of only those poems for which they felt genuine affinity.

With very few exceptions only new translations are included in this volume. A substantial number of these poems has never before been published in English translation.

The editors would like to think that this anthology has given an added impetus to translators who for some time have been attracted to German poetry but have hesitated to try their hand at an English version because of the slight chance that their efforts would see the light of day. The present volume, it is hoped, may lead the way to a second anthology to be devoted to German poetry of the twentieth-century.

We now release this 'cooperative anthology' to the public without unwarranted claims, but also without apologies for unavoidable imperfections. Creative translation is an unending endeavor – may the next translator testing his mettle on a poem included here achieve a fuller approximation. And may the reception of this volume prove also that many readers agree with our profound conviction that it was worth the effort of so many and that the effort should go on.

TABLE OF CONTENTS

U — U — U — U U — U —
U — U — U — U U — U —
U — U — U — U — U
— U U — U U — U — U

Nur einen Sommer gönnt, ihr Gewaltigen!
Und einen Herbst zu reifem Gesange mir,
Daß williger mein Herz, vom süßen
Spiele gesättigt, dann mir sterbe!

Die Seele, der im Leben ihr göttlich Recht
Nicht ward, sie ruht auch drunten im Orkus nicht;
Doch ist mir einst das Heilge, das am
Herzen mir liegt, das Gedicht, gelungen:

Willkommen dann, o Stille der Schattenwelt!
Zufrieden bin ich, wenn auch mein Saitenspiel
Mich nicht hinabgeleitet: einmal
Lebt ich wie Götter, und mehr bedarfs nicht.

A single summer grant me, ye Mighty Ones!,
And time wherein to harvest the ripened song,
That willingly my heart, thus slaked in
Rhythmical sweetness may heed the Summons.

The soul whose godlike due is denied it in
This life, finds no repose in the realm of shades.
Yet once the sacred trust I have at
Heart is accomplished – the poem spoken –

Be welcome then, O quiet land of death.
At peace I rest, albeit my lyre cannot
Go with me down to Orcus. Once I
Lived like the gods, and nought else is needed.

Der von Kürenberg

Ich zôch mir einen valken   mêre danne ein jâr.
Dô ich in gezamete   als ich in wolte hân
Und ich im sîn gevidere   mit golde wol bewant,
Er huop sich ûf vil hôhe   und fluog in anderiu lant.

Sît sach ich den valken   schône fliegen:
Er fuorte an sînem fuoze   sîdîne riemen,
Und was im sîn gevidere   alrôt guldîn.
Got sende si zesammen   die gern geliep wellen sin.

I reared me a falcon   longer than one year.
When I had tamed him   as I had willed him be
And I adorned his plumage   with a golden band,
He rose up most high   and flew to another land.

Since then I saw the falcon   grandly flying.
He wore on his foot   a silken ribbon.
The feathers of his wings   were golden fair.
May God bring them together   who fain would be a pair.

Alexander Gode

Unbekannter Dichter

Du bist mîn, ich bin dîn:
Des solt du gewis sîn.
Du bist beslozzen
In minem herzen;
Verlorn ist daz slüzzelîn:
Du muost immer drinne sîn.

I have thee, thou hast me.
Of this thou shalt assured be.
Thou art enlocked
In my heart.
Lost is the key:
Thou must forever in it be.

Alexander Gode

Heinrich von Morungen

Frouwe, wilt du mich genern,
Sô sich mich ein vil lützel an.
In mac mich langer niht erwern,
Den lîp muoz ich verloren hân.
Ich bin siech, mîn herze ist wunt.
Frouwe, daz hânt mir getân
Mîn ougen und dîn rôter munt.

Frouwe, mîne swêre sich,
Ê ich verliese mînen lîp.
Ein wort du sprêche wider mich:
Verkêre daz, du sêlic wip.
Sprichest iemer neinâ nein,
Daz brichet mir mîn herze enzwein.
Maht du doch etswan sprechen jâ,
Ja jâ ja jâ ja jâ jâ?
Daz lît mir an dem herzen nâ.

My Lady, if you'd have me whole
Let fall on me your glance so bright.
No longer master of my soul
I watch my life rush towards its night.
I sicken from a pain that rips
My heart. And what has caused my plight?
Why, my own eyes and your red lips.

My Lady, give heed to my plea
Before my life is fully spent.
The word that you have given me,
Reverse, sweet Lady, its intent.
You always tell me, "No, oh no,"
It breaks my heart when you speak so.
Why will you never tell me, "Yes,
Yes yes, yes yes, yes yes, and yes"?
That word would cure my heart's distress.

R. F. Trimble

Walther von der Vogelweide

Owê war sint verswunden   alliu mîniu jâr!
ist mir mîn leben getroumet,   oder ist ez wâr?
daz ich ie wânde ez wære,   was daz allez iht?
dar nâch hân ich geslâfen   und enweiz es niht.
nû bin ich erwachet,   und ist mir unbekant
daz mir hie vor was kûndic   als mîn ander hant.
liut unde lant, dar inn ich   von kinde bin erzogen,
die sint mir worden frömde   reht als ez sî gelogen.
die mîne gespilen wâren,   die sint træge unt alt.
unbereitet ist daz velt,   verhouwen ist der walt:
wan daz daz wazzer fliuzet   als ez wilent flôz,
für wâr mîn ungelücke   wânde ich wurde grôz.
mich grüezet maneger trâge,   der mich bekande ê wol.
diu welt ist allenthalben   ungenâden vol.
als ich gedenke an manegen   wünneclîchen tac
die mir sint enpfallen   als in daz mer ein slac,
iemer mêre ouwê.

Alas, whereto have vanished　　all my years!
Was, that I lived, but dreaming　　or is it true?
All that once seemed so real,　　was it so?
I fell asleep thereafter　　and now cannot recall.
I have of late awakened,　　and all is strange
That in my grasp I fancied　　like my other hand.
The people and lands among which　　from childhood I grew up
Bear alien looks as though　　it was all a lie.
The friends with whom I frolicked　　are old and slow.
Our fields lie untended,　　our trees long since are felled.
If not the brooks were flowing　　as they did of yore,
My haplessness, methinks,　　would be complete.
Many greet me vaguely　　who once knew me well.
The world is everywhere　　burdened with ungrace.
Alas, as I look back　　to the glorious days
That are gone as the splurge　　of a blow goes from the sea,
Alas, for ever more!

Janet Alison Livermore

Heinrich Albert

ABSCHIED

Gute Nacht, ihr mein Freund',
Ihr, o meine Lieben!
Alle, die ihr um mich weint,
Laßt euch nicht betrüben.
Diesen Abgang, den ich tu'
In die Erde nieder!
Schaut, die Sonne geht zur Ruh',
Kommt doch morgen wieder.

FAREWELL

Now, good night, my friends so dear,
Loves that I am leaving,
Who for me might spend a tear,
Do not think of grieving;
That I sink out of your sight
Is no cause for sorrow:
Look, the sun that sets tonight
Will come back tomorrow!

Martin Zwart

Johann von Rist

O EWIGKEIT, DU DONNERWORT

O Ewigkeit, du Donnerwort!
O Schwert, das durch die Seele bohrt!
O Anfang sonder Ende!
O Ewigkeit, Zeit ohne Zeit!
Ich weiß für große Traurigkeit
Nicht, wo ich mich hinwende!
Mein ganz erschrocknes Herz erbebt,
Daß mir die Zung am Gaumen klebt.

Kein Unglück ist in aller Welt,
Das endlich mit der Zeit nicht fällt
Und ganz wird aufgehoben;
Die Ewigkeit hat nur kein Ziel;
Sie treibet fort und fort ihr Spiel,
Läßt nimmer ab zu toben;
Ja, wie mein Heiland selber spricht,
Aus ihr ist kein Erlösung nicht.

O Ewigkeit, du machst mir bang!
O ewig, ewig ist zu lang:
Hier gilt fürwahr kein Scherzen.
Drum wenn ich diese lange Nacht
Zusamt der großen Pein betracht,
Erschreck ich recht von Herzen.
Nichts ist zu finden weit und breit
So schrecklich als die Ewigkeit!

ETERNITY TO COME

Eternity, you thunderword!
O sword that through my soul has bored!
Beginning without end!
The timeless time, eternity!
My great grief presses down on me,
I know not where to wend!
My whole astonished heart now heaves,
My tongue fast to my palate cleaves.

In all the world there is no pain
That time at last does not see wane,
Then disappear entirely.
Eternity alone lacks aim;
But on and on it plays its game,
From raging never free.
Yes, as my very Saviour teaches,
No one can escape its reaches.

Eternity, you fright my song!
Forever ever is too long;
A smile has no place here.
When I consider this great bane,
This long night of darkest pain,
My heart is chilled with fear.
Nothing is on land or sea
So dreadful as eternity!

Wach auf, o Mensch, vom Sündenschlaf!
Ermuntre dich, verlornes Schaf,
Und beßre bald dein Leben!
Wach auf! es ist doch hohe Zeit:
Es kommt heran die Ewigkeit,
Dir deinen Lohn zu geben!
Vielleicht ist heut der letzte Tag:
Wer weiß noch, wie man sterben mag?

O du verfluchtes Menschenkind,
Von Sinnen toll, von Herzen blind,
Laß ab, die Welt zu lieben!
Ach, ach, soll denn der Höllen Pein,
Da mehr denn tausend Henker sein,
Ohn Ende dich betrüben?
Wo lebt ein so beredter Mann,
Der dieses Werk aussprechen kann?

O Ewigkeit, du Donnerwort!
O Schwert, das durch die Seele bohrt!
O Anfang sonder Ende!
O Ewigkeit, Zeit ohne Zeit!
Ich weiß für große Traurigkeit
Nicht, wo ich mich hinwende!
Herr Jesu, wenn es dir gefällt,
Eil ich zu dir ins Himmelszelt.

Wake up, o Man, from sinner's sleep!
Rouse yourself, you wandering sheep,
You soon must change your way!
Wake up! the day is almost here:
Eternity is drawing near
To bring to you your pay.
Perhaps the world will end today;
Who knows death's hour or death's way?

O, accursed mortal child
Blind of heart, of senses wild,
Bid the world adieu!
O shall your pains in hell be more
Than thousand torturers could pour
In centuries on you?
Where lives a man so eloquent,
Who could describe such cruel lament!

Eternity, you thunderword!
O sword that through my soul has bored!
Beginning without end!
The timeless time, eternity!
My great grief presses down on me,
I know not where to wend!
O, if it please Thee, Lord, I'll fly
To Thee and Thine, beyond the sky.

Robert Kramer

Paul Gerhardt

Geh aus, mein Herz, und suche Freud'
In dieser lieben Sommerzeit
An deines Gottes Gaben:
Schau an der schönen Gärten Zier,
Und siehe, wie sie mir und dir
Sich ausgeschmücket haben.

Die Bäume stehen voller Laub,
Das Erdreich decket seinen Staub
Mit einem grünen Kleide:
Narzissus und die Tulipan,
Die ziehen sich viel schöner an
Als Salomonis Seide.

Die Lerche schwingt sich in die Luft,
Das Täublein fleucht aus seiner Kluft
Und macht sich in die Wälder.
Die hochbegabte Nachtigall
Ergetzt und füllt mit ihrem Schall
Berg, Hügel, Tal und Felder.

Die Glucke führt ihr Völklein aus,
Der Storch baut und bewohnt sein Haus,
Das Schwälblein speist die Jungen.
Der schnelle Hirsch, das leichte Reh
Ist froh und kommt aus seiner Höh
Ins tiefe Gras gesprungen.

Go out in this dear summertide
And seek to find the joys that bide
In Heaven's gifts, oh heart:
Behold the gardens' lovely hue,
And see how they for me and you
Are decked by fairest art.

The trees in fullest leafage rise,
The earth, to give its dust disguise,
Has put a green dress on.
Narcissus and the tulip-bloom
Far finer vestment do assume
Than silks of Solomon.

The lark soars high into the air,
The little dove departs its lair
And takes the woodland's way.
The sweetly gifted nightingale
Fills hill and mountain, field and dale
With song, and makes them gay.

The hen leads out her little troop,
The stork does build and fill his stoop,
Its young the swallow feeds.
The hasty stag, the agile doe
Are glad, and from their heights do go
A-running through the reeds.

Die Bächlein rauschen in dem Sand
Und malen sich und ihren Rand
Mit schattenreichen Myrthen.
Die Wiesen liegen hart dabei
Und klingen ganz von Lustgeschrei
Der Schaf' und ihrer Hirten.

Die unverdroßne Bienenschar
Zeucht hin und her, sucht hier und daar
Ihr edle Honigspeise.
Des süßen Weinstocks starker Saft
Kriegt täglich neue Stärk und Kraft
In seinem schwachen Reise.

Der Weizen wächset mit Gewalt,
Darüber jauchzet Jung und Alt
Und rühmt die große Güte
Des, der so überflüssig labt
Und mit so manchem Gut begabt
Das menschliche Gemüte.

Ich selbsten kann und mag nicht ruhn,
Des großen Gottes großes Tun
Erweckt mir alle Sinnen.
Ich singe mit, wenn alles singt,
Und lasse, was dem Höchsten klingt,
Aus meinem Herze rinnen.

The brooklets rustle in the sand
And o'er them and their banks a band
Of shady myrtles keep.
The meadowlands lie close thereby,
Resounding from the happy cry
Of shepherds and their sheep.

The bee-host back and forth has made
Its trips, thus seeking unafraid
Its noble honey-food.
The goodly vine, with juice grown big,
Gets daily in its weakest sprig
Its strength and force renewed.

The wheat grows large with all its might,
And does both young and old delight:
They sing the bounteousness
Of Him Who soothes so generously
And does such countless property
Upon man's spirit press.

Now I can neither rest, nor will:
Great God's great manufactures thrill
Awake my every sense.
I sing along, when all does sing,
And let what shall to Heaven ring
From out my heart commence.

George C. Schoolfield

Paul Fleming

AN SICH

Sei dennoch unverzagt, gib dennoch unverloren,
Weich keinem Glücke nicht, steh höher als der Neid,
Vergnüge dich an dir und achte für kein Leid,
Hat sich gleich wider dich Glück, Ort und Zeit verschworen.

Was dich betrübt und labt, halt alles für erkoren,
Nimm dein Verhängnis an, laß alles unbereut,
Tu, was getan muß sein, und eh man dirs gebeut.
Was du noch hoffen kannst, das wird noch stets geboren.

Was klagt, was lobt man doch? Sein Unglück und sein Glücke
Ist ihm ein jeder selbst. Schau alle Sachen an.
Dies alles ist in dir, laß deinen eiteln Wahn,

Und eh du förder gehst, so geh in dich zurücke.
Wer sein selbst Meister ist und sich beherrschen kann,
Dem ist die weite Welt und alles untertan.

TO HIMSELF

Yet do not be afraid, yet give no post forlorn,
Rise over jealousy, and to each joy assent,
Think it no ill but stay with your own self content,
If fortune, place, and time 'gainst you a league have sworn.

Assume that all has plan, if it do sooth or scorn,
Accept your fate and leave each deed without repent,
What must be done, that do, ere orders speed event.
Whate'er you still can hope, can each day still be born.

Why do men mourn or praise? His fortune, weal or woe,
Is each man to himself. Into each thing inquire –
All this resides in you. Your vain dreams let expire,

And go into yourself, before you farther go:
Who's master of himself and rules his own desire
Has subject unto him the mighty globe entire.

George C. Schoolfield

Andreas Gryphius

ABEND

Der schnelle Tag ist hin; die Nacht schwingt ihre Fahn
Und führt die Sternen auf. Der Menschen müde Scharen
Verlassen Feld und Werk; wo Tier und Vögel waren,
Traurt itzt die Einsamkeit. Wie ist die Zeit vertan!

Der Port naht mehr und mehr sich zu der Glieder Kahn.
Gleichwie dies Licht verfiel, so wird in wenig Jahren
Ich, du, und was man hat, und was man sieht, hinfahren.
Dies Leben kömmt mir vor als eine Rennebahn.

Laß, höchster Gott, mich doch nicht auf dem Laufplatz gleiten!
Laß mich nicht Ach, nicht Pracht, nicht Lust, nicht Angst verleiten
Dein ewig, heller Glanz sei vor und neben mir!

Laß, wenn der müde Leib entschläft, die Seele wachen,
Und wenn der letzte Tag wird mit mir Abend machen,
So reiß mich aus dem Tal der Finsternis zu dir!

EVENING

The rapid day is gone; her banner swings the night,
And leads the stars aloft. Men's wearied hosts have wended
Away from fields and work; where beast and bird attended,
Now solitude laments. How vain has been time's flight!

The vessel of our limbs draws nearer to the bight.
In but a little while, just as this light descended,
Will I, you, what we have, and what we see be ended.
E'en as a runner's track seems life within my sight.

Great God, grant me that I in coursing do not blunder!
Nor joy trick me nor fear nor woe nor earthly wonder!
Let Your unfailing light my comrade be and guide!

When my tired body sleeps, grant that my soul be waking,
And when the final day my eventide is making,
Then take me from this vale of darkness to Your side!

George C. Schoolfield

EITELKEIT DER WELT

Du siehst, wohin du siehst, nur Eitelkeit auf Erden.
Was dieser heute baut, reißt jener morgen ein;
Wo jetzund Städte stehn, wird eine Wiese sein,
Auf der ein Schäferkind wird spielen mit den Herden.

Was jetzund prächtig blüht, soll bald zertreten werden;
Was jetzt so pocht und trotzt, ist morgen Asch' und Bein;
Nichts ist, das ewig sei, kein Erz, kein Marmorstein.
Jetzt lacht das Glück uns an, bald donnern die Beschwerden.

Der hohen Taten Ruhm muß wie ein Traum vergehn.
Soll denn das Spiel der Zeit der leichte Mensch bestehn?
Ach, was ist alles dies, was wir für köstlich achten,

Als schlechte Nichtigkeit, als Schatten, Staub und Wind,
Als eine Wiesenblum', die man nicht wieder findt!
Noch will, was ewig ist, kein einig Mensch betrachten.

ALL IS VANITY

You see, where'er you look, on earth but vainness' hour.
Tomorrow will destroy that which was built today;
The meadow where the boy a-shepherding will play
Together with his flock, there now the cities tower.

That will be trampled soon which now is full in flower,
The morrow's ash and bone do now defiance inveigh;
No bronze nor marble stands that will not pass away.
Now fortune laughs, but we are soon in hardship's power.

The fame of noble deeds must like a dream desist,
Shall then the toy of time, inconstant man, persist?
Oh, what are all these things for which we long endeavor

But wretched nothingness, but wind and dust and shade,
A flower of the field from which our eyes have strayed!
Yet no man contemplates what will endure for ever.

                                        George C. Schoolfield

MENSCHLICHES ELENDE

(*original spelling preserved*)

Was sind wir menschen doch! ein wohnhaus grimmer schmertzen,
Ein ball des falschen glücks, ein irrlicht dieser zeit,
Ein schauplatz herber angst, besetzt mit scharffem leid,
Ein bald verschmeltzter schnee und abgebrannte kertzen.

Diss leben fleucht davon wie ein geschwätz und schertzen.
Die vor uns abgelegt des schwachen leibes kleid
Und in das todten-buch der grossen sterbligkeit
Längst eingeschrieben sind, sind uns aus sinn und hertzen.

Gleich wie ein eitel traum leicht aus der acht hinfällt
Und wie ein strom verscheusst, den keine macht auffhält,
So muss auch unser nahm, lob, ehr und ruhm verschwinden.

Was itzund athem holt, muss mit der lufft entfliehn,
Was nach uns kommen wird, wird uns ins grab nachziehn.
Was sag ich? wir vergehn, wie rauch von starcken winden.

HUMAN MISERY

What are we men indeed? Grim torment's habitation,
A toy of fickle luck, wisp in time's wilderness,
A scene of bitter fear and filled with keen distress,
And tapers burned to stubs, snow's quick evaporation.

This life does flee away like jest or conversation;
Those who before us laid aside the body's dress
And in the domesday-book of monster mortalness
Old entry found, have left our mind's and heart's sensation.

Just as an empty dream from notice lightly flees,
And as a stream is lost whose course no might may cease,
So must our honor, fame, our praise and name be ended.

What presently draws breath, must perish with the air,
What after us will come, someday our grave will share.
What do I say? We pass as smoke on strong winds wended.

George C. Schoolfield

TRÄNEN DES VATERLANDES

Wir sind doch nunmehr ganz, ja mehr denn ganz verheeret!
Der frechen Völker Schar, die rasende Posaun,
Das vom Blut fette Schwert, die donnernde Kartaun
Hat aller Schweiß und Fleiß und Vorrat aufgezehret.

Die Türme stehn in Glut, die Kirch ist umgekehret,
Das Rathaus liegt im Graus, die Starken sind zerhaun,
Die Jungfraun sind geschändt, und wo wir hin nur schaun,
Ist Feuer, Pest und Tod, der Herz und Geist durchfähret.

Hier durch die Schanz und Stadt rinnt allzeit frisches Blut.
Dreimal sind schon sechs Jahr, als unser Ströme Flut,
Von Leichen fast verstopft, sich langsam fortgedrungen.

Doch schweig ich noch von dem, was ärger als der Tod,
Was grimmer denn die Pest und Glut und Hungersnot:
Daß auch der Seelenschatz so vielen abgezwungen.

GRABSCHRIFT MARIANAE GRYPHIAE, SEINES BRUDERN PAULI TÖCHTERLEIN

Geboren in der Flucht, umringt mit Schwert und Brand,
Schier in dem Rauch erstickt, der Mutter herbes Pfand,
Des Vaters höchste Furcht, die an das Licht gedrungen,
Als die ergrimmte Glut mein Vaterland verschlungen:
Ich habe diese Welt beschaut und bald gesegnet,
Weil mir auf einen Tag all' Angst der Welt begegnet:
Wo ihr die Tage zählt, so bin ich jung verschwunden,
Sehr alt, wofern ihr schätzt, was ich für Angst empfunden.

TEARS OF THE FATHERLAND

Entire, more than entire have we been devastated!
The maddened clarion, the bold invaders' horde,
The mortar thunder-voiced, the blood-anointed sword
Have all men's sweat and work and store annihilated.

The towers stand in flames, the church is violated,
The strong are massacred, a ruin our council board,
Our maidens raped, and where my eyes have scarce explored
Fire, pestilence, and death my heart have dominated.

Here through the moat and town runs always new-let blood,
And for three-times-six years our very rivers' flood
With corpses choked has pressed ahead in tedious measure;

I shall not speak of that which is still worse than death,
And crueller than the plague and torch and hunger's breath:
From many has been forced even the spirit's treasure.

George C. Schoolfield

EPITAPH FOR MARIANA,
HIS BROTHER PAUL'S LITTLE DAUGHTER

Born during flight, circled by sword and fire.
In smoke I almost stifled. My mother's bitter burden,
My father's greatest fear which pressed towards the light
While sweeping, raging fire consumed my fatherland.
I looked upon this world, soon said farewell to it,
For in one day I met all earthly agonies.
If you but count my days, I was young when I died,
But think of all my fears: How old I died! How old!

Gertrude C. Schwebell

ÜBER DIE GEBURT CHRISTI, 1657

Kind! Dreimal süßes Kind! In was bedrängten Nöten
Bricht dein Geburtstag ein! Der Engel Scharen Macht
Bejauchzet deine Kripp' und singt bei stiller Nacht;
Die Hirten preisen dich mit hellgestimmten Flöten.

Ach um mich klingt der Hall der rasenden Trompeten,
Der rauhe Paukenklang, der Büchsen Donner kracht.
Du schläfst, der tolle Grimm der schnellen Zwietracht wacht
Und dräut mit Stahl und Schwert und Flamm und Haß und Töten.

O Friedefürst! Lach uns aus deinen Windeln an!
Daß mein bestürztes Herz, das nichts als seufzen kann,
Dir auch ein Freudenlied, o Sohn der Jungfrau! bringe.

Doch wenn ich, Gott! durch dich mit Gott in Friede steh,
So kann ich fröhlich sein, ob auch die Welt vergeh,
Indem du in mir ruhst. O Kind! mein Wunsch gelinge!

CONCERNING THE BIRTH OF CHRIST, 1657

Child! Three-times blessed child! In what afflicted ages
Your natal day has dawned! The angel-squadron's might
Your manger celebrates and sings by stilly night,
The shepherd in your praise his bright-voiced flute engages.

Oh, round me rings the cry of trumpets in their rages,
The kettledrum's rough noise, the guns do thunder smite.
You sleep; but yonder wakes swift discord's crazy blight,
And steel and sword and flame and hate and death presages.

Oh prince of peace! To us smile from your swaddling clothes!
That my poor heart, which naught but sighing knows,
May bring you, maiden's son, a song of jubilation.

Yet if I, God, through You may stand in peace,
Then I can still rejoice, although the world may cease,
Since You abide with me. Child, hear my supplication!

George C. Schoolfield

Christian Hoffmann von Hoffmannswaldau

Wo sind die Stunden
Der süßen Zeit,
Da ich zuerst empfunden,
Wie deine Lieblichkeit
Mich dir verbunden?
Sie sind verrauscht. Es bleibet doch dabei,
Daß alle Lust vergänglich sei.

Das reine Scherzen,
So mich ergetzt
Und in dem tiefen Herzen
Sein Merkmal eingesetzt,
Läßt mich in Schmerzen.
Du hast mir mehr als deutlich kundgetan,
Daß Freundlichkeit nicht ankern kann.

Empfangene Küsse,
Ambrierter Saft,
Verbleibt nicht lange süße
Und kommt von aller Kraft;
Verrauschte Flüsse
Erquicken nicht. Was unsern Geist erfreut
Entspringt aus Gegenwärtigkeit.

Ich schwamm in Freude,
Der Liebe Hand
Spann mir ein Kleid von Seide;
Das Blatt hat sich gewandt,
Ich geh im Leide,
Ich wein itzund, daß Lieb und Sonnenschein
Stets voller Angst und Wolken sein.

So sweet, so golden,
Where is the time
When I came first to bolden
And own your beauty's prime
Had me beholden?
It pearled away, as though again to show
That earthly joys which come, must go.

Your plesantnesses,
So arch, so fleet,
Which in my heart's recesses
Found permanent retreat
Have brought distresses.
You more than clearly made me understand
That friendliness is drifting sand.

A kiss's flavor,
Its perfumed taste,
Keeps not for long its savor
And quickly goes to waste.
An emptied quaver
Is little use. For hearts to gather force,
A presentness must be the source.

I swam in pleasure;
The hand of love
Dressed me in silk to measure.
But pain, decreed above,
Fills now my leisure;
And I bewail that love and sunny skies
Prepare for heavy clouds and sighs.

Alexander Gode

VERGÄNGLICHKEIT DER SCHÖNHEIT

Es wird der bleiche Tod mit seiner kalten Hand
Dir endlich mit der Zeit um deine Brüste streichen,
Der liebliche Korall der Lippen wird verbleichen;
Der Schultern warmer Schnee wird werden kalter Sand.

Der Augen süßer Blitz, die Kräfte deiner Hand,
Für welchen solches fällt, die werden zeitlich weichen.
Das Haar, das itzund kann des Goldes Glanz erreichen,
Tilgt endlich Tag and Jahr als ein gemeines Band.

Der wohlgesetzte Fuß, die lieblichen Gebärden,
Die werden teils zu Staub, teils nichts und nichtig werden,
Dann opfert keiner mehr der Gottheit deiner Pracht.

Dies und noch mehr als dies muß endlich untergehen.
Dein Herze kann allein zu aller Zeit bestehen,
Dieweil es die Natur aus Diamant gemacht.

BEAUTY'S TRANSITORINESS

Then pallid death at last will with his icy hand,
Where time hides in the palm, your lovely breasts contain;
The coral of your lips will from its beauty wane,
Your shoulders' warmth of snow will change to icy sand.

Sweet lightning of your eyes, the powers of your hand
That you such conquests make, will but brief hours remain.
Your locks, which presently the glance of gold attain,
The day and year at last will ruin in common band.

Your well-placed foot will then, your movements in their grace,
To naught and nothing part, and part to dust give place.
Before your splendor's god no offering more is laid.

This and still more than this at last must pass away.
Your heart alone has strength its constant self to stay,
Since nature this same heart of diamond has made.

George C. Schoolfield

Philip von Zesen

ABENDLIED

Es hat nun mehr das güldne Licht
Des Himmels seinen Lauf verricht,
Der Tag hat sich geneiget;
Der blasse Mond steht auf der Wacht,
Die Sterne leuchten durch die Nacht,
Der süße Schlaf sich zeiget.

Ei, nun will ich in sanfter Ruh
Die Nacht mit Schlafen bringen zu,
Ermüdet durch viel Schreiben,
Das durch den langen Tag ich trieb,
Bis mir die Nacht den Paß verhieb,
Die Sinnen fort zu treiben.

Indessen sei mein Glanz und Licht
Dein freudenreiches Angesicht,
O Sonne meiner Seelen,
Daß nicht der Nächte Schatten mich
Mit Furcht und Schrecken inniglich
Im Herzen möge quälen.

Nimm weg den schweren Sündenschwall,
So sich ereignet überall,
Aus meines Herzens Schranken.
Daß ich fein sanfte ruhen mag,
Und, wann nun kömmt der frühe Tag,
Dir, Höchster, freudig danken.

Hiermit will ich nun schlafen ein
Und dir, o Gott, ergeben sein.
Du wirst mich wohl erretten.
Behüte mich für schnellem Tod,
Für aller Angst und Krieges Not
Und für des Teufels Ketten.

EVENING SONG

The golden light has presently
Its coursing through the sky let be;
The day its kingdom ends.
The pale moon keeps its sentry post,
Through darkness shines the starry host,
And gentle sleep descends.

Oh, I shall now in sweet repose
See how the night in slumber goes,
Exhausted by my pen,
With which throughout the day I strove,
Until the fall of darkness drove
My senses from their ken.

But let my glow, my flame advance
From out your joyful countenance,
Oh sunlight of my soul,
That not the shadows of the night
With terror make and cozy fright
My heart a torture-hole.

Remove that heavy swell of sin,
Which everywhere has entered in,
From my heart's bounds away,
That I may sweetly sleep, and that
I thank You, Lord, all joyful at
The coming of the day.

Now I shall lay me down to sleep
And give my soul, God, to your keep,
Which surely you will save.
Protect me from a hasty death,
From terror and from war's cruel breath,
Nor make me Satan's slave.

George C. Schoolfield

Catharina Regina von Greiffenberg

GOTT LOBENDE FRÜHLINGSLUST. SONNENLOB
(*original spelling preserved*)

Du Sternen-Kaiserin / des Himmels werte Krone /
Das Aug der großen Welt / der ganzen Erde Seel /
Der Strahlen Mittelpunkt / die Lust- und Schönheit-Quell /
Das Leben aller Ding / der Klarheit Strahlen Throne /

Du Leut-Erleuchterin / du Schatzhaus aller Wonne /
Des Höchsten Spiegelglas / (nichts zeigt ihn also hell) /
Der stäten Regung Bild durch deine schnelle Schnell' /
Du goldner Wunderbrunn / du sonderliche Sonne!

Ein Schiff / auf dem uns Gott die Lebensgüter schickt /
Sein Wagen / der zu uns den Himmels-Segen führet /
Der Zeiten König bist / der Tag und Jahr regieret /

Des edle Gegenwart die Länder sehr erquickt /
Du schöner Segenbaum / den Gottes Hand gepflanzet /
Aus deiner Strahlen-Blüh des Schöpfers Schönheit glanzet.

SPRING-JOY PRAISING GOD. PRAISE OF THE SUN

You empress of the stars, the heavens' worthy crown,
The world's great eye, and soul of all the spreading earth,
The middle-point of beams and joy's and beauty's birth,
The life of every thing and clarity's bright throne.

Folk's flame and treasure-house, from which all bliss is won,
God's mirror (for naught else can show His lustre's worth),
Eternal motion's show in your hot hastening girth,
You golden wonder-fount, incomparable sun!

A ship, which brings to us from God life's needed wares,
His wagon, which to us the heavens' crop relays,
You are the king of time, and rule the years and days.

Your noble presence well the continents repairs,
You lovely blessings-tree, set down by God's designs,
From out your bloom of light the Maker's beauty shines.

George C. Schoolfield

August Adolf von Haugwitz

AN SIE UMB EINEN KUSS
(*original spelling preserved*)

Der Glantz / der Blitz / die Gluth / die Flammen deiner Augen
Hat mich erschreckt / verblendt / entbrandt und angezündt /
Und einen Durst erweckt / den Hertz und Seel empfindt /
So / dass kein Wasser mehr zum leschen mir wil taugen /

Auch selbst der Thränen nicht so bitter heisse Laugen /
Die doch stets überhäufft aus meinen Augen rinnt /
Und meine Wangen netzt. Drum allerliebstes Kind
Lass mich den Honig-Thau von deinen Lippen saugen /

Der einig ists der mir die heissen Schmertzen kühlt.
Die mein entbrandte Seel' und rauchend Hertze fühlt.
Was seumst du? lesche doch / ach lesche doch geshwind

Den Schmertz / den Durst / den Brandt / das Feuer / diese Hitze /
Den deiner Augen Glantz / und Gluth / und Flamm / und Blitze
Erweckt / ansteckt / gemacht und in mir angezündt.

TO HER FOR A KISS

The shine, the bolt, the glow, the bright flame of your eye
Have frightened, blinded me, enflamed and set alight,
And have awakened thirsts that heart and soul excite,
So that no water can my burning pacify,

Nor e'en the tears themselves, their hot and bitter lye,
Which flows in mighty flood forever from my sight
And irrigates my cheeks. So, child of my delight,
Allow that I your lips of honey-dew suck dry,

For it alone can cool the hot pains of desire,
Which fill my smoking heart, my spirit in its fire.
Why do you hesitate? Drown, drown with all your speed

The pain, the thirst, the flare, the fire-brand, and this heat,
Which your eye's shine and glow and flame and lightning sheet
Awaken, kindle, make, and deep within me breed.

George C. Schoolfield

Christian Friedrich Hunold

ÜBER DIE ZEIT

(*original spelling preserved*)

Ein Pfeil geht zwar geschwind / die Luft saust schnell vorbey /
Die Wolcken lauffen sehr / der Blitz fährt in die Eichen /
Sprich / ob was schnellers noch / als seine Strahlen sey?
Blitz / Pfeil / Lufft / Wolcken sind der Zeit nicht zu
    vergleichen.
Sie streicht geschwind dahin / kein Auge kan es sehn:
Meer / Wind und Wetter sind von Menschen aufzuhalten/
Die Zeit von keinem nicht: sie lässt auch Käyser stehn/
Nicht über einen Blick vermag ein Fürst zu walten.
Wer kauffte nicht die Zeit vor Millionen ein?
Doch geht sie / weil sie mehr als gülden ist zu schätzen. /
Wer sich der Zeit bedient / kan reich in Armuth seyn. /
Bey zeiten kan die Zeit in Glück und Ehren setzen.
Drum edle Menschen braucht anitzt der edlen Zeit;
Gar lange wird der Sand nicht in dem Glase bleiben;
Und sucht die Weissheit mehr als die Ergötzlichkeit /
Vertreibt die Zeit doch nicht / sie wird sich selbst vertreiben.

CONCERNING TIME

An arrow's quick indeed, swift swirls away the air,
The clouds fly on apace, and oak the lightning sears:
Say, whether aught in speed can with its flames compare?
Bolt, arrow, air, and cloud are not the instant's peers.
Time rushes quickly by, no eye its flight intrudes.
Sea, wind, and weather are by men to be delayed,
But time is stopped by none: it emperors eludes,
Not e'en a second can by mighty prince be stayed.
Who would not millions give for time as recompense?
Yet it flies on, since it with more than gold is fraught.
Whoe'er makes use of time has wealth in indigence.
Betimes are men by time to luck and honor brought.
Thus, noble men, do now your noble time employ,
Since sand will not remain for long within the glass;
Seek after wisdom more than you seek after joy,
Make time not pass away: it of itself will pass.

George C. Schoolfield

Johann Christian Günther

TROSTARIA

Endlich bleibt nicht ewig aus,
Endlich wird der Trost erscheinen;
Endlich grünt der Hoffnungsstrauß,
Endlich hört man auf zu weinen,
Endlich bricht der Thränenkrug,
Endlich spricht der Tod: Genug!

Endlich wird aus Wasser Wein,
Endlich kommt die rechte Stunde,
Endlich fällt der Kerker ein,
Endlich heilt die tiefe Wunde.
Endlich macht die Sklaverei
Den gefangnen Joseph frei.

Endlich, endlich kann der Neid,
Endlich auch Herodes sterben;
Endlich Davids Hirtenkleid
Seinen Saum in Purpur färben.
Endlich macht die Zeit den Saul
Zur Verfolgung schwach und faul.

Endlich nimmt der Lebenslauf
Unsres Elends auch ein Ende;
Endlich steht ein Heiland auf,
Der das Joch der Knechtschaft wende;
Endlich machen vierzig Jahr
Die Verheißung zeitig wahr.

Endlich blüht die Aloe,
Endlich trägt der Palmbaum Früchte;
Endlich schwindet Furcht und Weh,
Endlich wird der Schmerz zu nichte;
Endlich sieht man Freudental;
Endlich, Endlich kommt einmal.

CONSOLATION-ARIA

Finally stays no more away,
Finally balm its pledge will keep,
Finally burgeons hope's bouquet,
Finally man will cease to weep,
Finally will the tear-jug break,
Finally death its share forsake.

Finally water turns to wine,
Finally will the right hour peal,
Finally falls the vault's confine,
Finally gaping wounds will heal,
Finally will that slavery
Turn imprisoned Joseph free.

Finally can e'en jealousness,
Finally can e'en Herod end,
Finally David's shepherd-dress
Can its hem to purple lend.
Finally Saul, by time made weak,
Will no more his quarry seek.

Finally will the life-long sum
Of our woes an ending take,
Finally will that savior come
Who our serfdom's yoke can break,
Finally forty years' accrue
Timely makes the promise true.

Finally will the aloe bloom,
Finally will the palm bear fruit,
Finally fear must pass, and gloom,
Finally pain is destitute,
Finally joy's demesne we see,
Finally will some morrow be.

George C. Schoolfield

Matthias Claudius

DIE MUTTER BEI DER WIEGE

Schlaf, süßer Knabe, süß und mild!
Du deines Vaters Ebenbild!
Das bist du; zwar dein Vater spricht,
Du habest seine Nase nicht.

Nur eben itzo war er hier
Und sah dir ins Gesicht
Und sprach: „Viel hat er zwar von mir,
Doch meine Nase nicht."

Mich dünkt es selbst, sie ist zu klein,
Doch muß es seine Nase sein;
Denn wenn's nicht seine Nase wär',
Wo hätt'st du denn die Nase her?

Schlaf, Knabe, was dein Vater spricht,
Spricht er wohl nur im Scherz;
Hab' immer seine Nase nicht
Und habe nur sein Herz!

THE MOTHER BY THE CRADLE

Sleep, darling boy, so sweet and mild!
The image of your father, child,
That's what you are; though he insist
That in your face his nose was missed.

And here just now he chanced to be,
And looked into your face,
And said: "He has a lot of me,
But of my nose, no trace".

It is too small, it seems to me,
And yet his nose 'tis sure to be;
For if this proves to be untrue,
How did it come to be with you?

Sleep, son, the things your father says
Are said in jesting part;
You need not ever have his nose,
But only have his heart!

D. G. Wright

Der Sämann säet den Samen,
Die Erde empfängt ihn, und über ein kleines
Keimet die Blume herauf –

Du liebtest sie. Was auch dies Leben
Sonst für Gewinn hat, war klein dir geachtet,
Und sie entschlummerte dir.

Was weinest du neben dem Grabe
Und hebst die Hände zur Wolke des Todes
Und der Verwesung empor?

Wie Gras auf dem Felde sind Menschen
Dahin, wie Blätter, nur wenige Tage
Gehn wir verkleidet einher!

Der Adler besuchet die Erde,
Doch säumt nicht, schüttelt vom Flügel den Staub und
Kehret zur Sonne zurück.

The seed the sower is sowing.
The earth receives it, and after a short while
Upwards the flower then grows.

You have loved her. Whatever else life can
give, very little regard you had for it,
and she forever is gone.

Why then by the grave are you weeping
and to the cloud of decay and of death are
you here thus lifting your hands?

Like grass in the field wither humans
away, like leaves, and for only a few days
we go about in disguise.

To visit the earth comes the eagle,
but tarries not, from his wings shakes the dust and
towards the sun he returns.

Dorothea M. Singer

PHIDILE

Ich war erst sechzehn Sommer alt,
Unschuldig und nichts weiter,
Und kannte nichts als unsern Wald,
Als Blumen, Gras und Kräuter.

Da kam ein fremder Jüngling her;
Ich hatt' ihn nicht verschrieben,
Und wußte nicht, wohin noch her;
Der kam und sprach von Lieben.

Er hatte schönes langes Haar
Um seinen Nacken wehen;
Und einen Nacken, als der war,
Hab' ich noch nie gesehen.

Sein Auge, himmelblau und klar!
Schien freundlich was zu flehen;
So blau und freundlich, als das war,
Hab' ich noch keins gesehen.

Und sein Gesicht, wie Milch und Blut!
Ich hab's nie so gesehen;
Auch, was er sagte, war sehr gut,
Nur konnt' ich's nicht verstehen.

Er ging mir allenthalben nach
Und drückte mir die Hände,
Und sagte immer O und Ach
Und küßte sie behende.

Ich sah ihn einmal freundlich an
Und fragte, was er meinte;

PHIDILE

I was but sixteen summers old,
All innocence, all wonder . . .
I knew our pasture, knew our world,
But knew of nothing yonder.

Then, from afar, there came a lad.
It was not I who spelled him.
Whatever goal his journey had,
He stayed and said love held him.

He had long lovely silken hair
About his neck a-blowing.
And such a neck! – I've seen not e'er
A neck like that a-growing.

His eyes seemed bluer than the skies
And full of kind endeavor.
Such blue and kind and begging eyes
I had not seen, not ever.

Oh, and his face! Blood-red, milk-white!
I'd seen none such, not ever!
And all he said was true, was right!
For me, though, 't was too clever.

He followed me where'er I went
And took my hands and pressed them
And seemed with Ah's and Oh's all spent
And kissed my hands and blessed them.

Then once, not meaning any harm,
I asked why he was sighing,

Da fiel der junge schöne Mann
Mir um den Hals, und weinte.

Das hatte niemand noch getan;
Doch war's mir nicht zuwider,
Und meine beiden Augen sahn
In meinen Busen nieder.

Ich sagt' ihm nicht ein einzig Wort,
Als ob ich's übel nähme,
Kein einzigs, und – er flohe fort;
Wenn er doch wieder käme!

Whereat my fair lad put his arm
Around me and – was crying.

Such like no one had ever done,
And yet, I did not mind it.
My eyes looked for a place to run
But somehow could not find it.

No single word in what I said
Could mean I was offended.
Not one! But up my lad and fled.
Would he came back! God lend it!

Alexander Gode

DER TOD UND DAS MÄDCHEN

Das Mädchen:

Vorüber! Ach vorüber!
Geh, wilder Knochenmann!
Ich bin noch jung, geh, Lieber!
Und rühre mich nicht an.

Der Tod:

Gib deine Hand, du schön und zart Gebild!
Bin Freund und komme nicht zu strafen.
Sei gutes Muts! ich bin nicht wild,
Sollst sanft in meinen Armen schlafen!"

DEATH AND THE MAIDEN

The maiden:
Pass by me, go, and hie thee
oh, fearsome skeleton!
I am still young! Pass by me,
dear, touch me not, pass on!

Death:
Give me your hand, you lovely, tender maid!
As friend I come, to punish never.
Fearsome I'm not! Be unafraid!
Sleep softly in my arms forever!

Dorothea M. Singer

KRIEGSLIED

'S ist Krieg! 's ist Krieg! O Gottes Engel wehre
Und rede Du darein!
'S ist leider Krieg – und ich begehre
Nicht schuld daran zu sein!

Was sollt ich machen, wenn im Schlaf mit Grämen
Und blutig, bleich und blaß
Die Geister der Erschlagnen zu mir kämen
Und vor mir weinten, was?

Wenn wackre Männer, die sich Ehre suchten,
Verstümmelt und halb tot
Im Staub sich vor mir wälzten und mir fluchten
In ihrer Todesnot?

Wenn tausend, tausend Väter, Mütter, Bräute,
So glücklich vor dem Krieg,
Nun alle elend, alle arme Leute,
Wehklagten über mich?

Wenn Hunger, böse Seuch und ihre Nöten
Freund, Freund und Feind ins Grab
Versammleten und mir zu Ehren krähten
Von einer Leich herab?

Was hülf mir Kron und Land und Gold und Ehre?
Die könnten mich nicht freun!
S' ist leider Krieg – und ich begehre
Nicht schuld daran zu sein!

A SONG OF WAR

The world's at war! O powers above, conspire
To quench the hideous flame!
Alas the war! And I may but desire
That mine be not the blame.

What should I do, if in my dreams the slaughtered
Pale rising should appear,
Bloody accusing ghosts, and silent watered
My bed with many a tear?

If good men, whom my cruel will coerces,
Maimed, wounded unto death,
Should writhe before me in the mire, with curses
Upon their dying breath?

If all these thousands, children, fathers, mothers,
Once happy, sheltered, fed,
Now wretched all, poor people, for those others
Cried woe upon my head?

If want and horror, pestilence, starvation,
Once their dread work were done,
Should gather friend and foe in execration
Of me, the guilty one?

What worth all power to which I might aspire,
The glory and acclaim?
Alas the war! And I may but desire
That mine be not the blame.

Albert Bloch

BEI DEM GRABE MEINES VATERS

Friede sei um diesen Grabstein her!
Sanfter Friede Gottes! Ach, sie haben
Einen guten Mann begraben,
Und mir war er mehr;

Träufte mir von Segen, dieser Mann,
Wie ein milder Stern aus bessern Welten!
Und ich kanns ihm nicht vergelten,
Was er mir getan.

Er entschlief; sie gruben ihn hier ein.
Leiser, süßer Trost, von Gott gegeben,
Und ein Ahnden von dem ew'gen Leben
Düft' um sein Gebein!

Bis ihn Jesus Christus, groß und hehr!
Freundlich wird erwecken – ach, sie haben
Einen guten Mann begraben,
Und mir war er mehr.

AT THE GRAVE OF MY FATHER

Peace shall ever by this tombstone be!
Godsent, gentle peace! Oh, to his grave
They bore him who goodness gave —
And much more to me.

Deeds so richly bless'd this man has done,
As a star from better worlds is lighting!
And the hope of my requiting
All his love is gone.

He passed on; they lay him in the ground.
May the peace and calm God is providing,
Dreams of love for evermore abiding
Drift about his mound.

Till Lord Jesus Christ — Sublime is He! —
Kindly wakens him. Oh, to his grave
They bore one who goodness gave —
And much more to me.

Dorothea M. Singer

Johann Gottfried Herder

Ein Traum, ein Traum ist unser Leben
Auf Erden hier.

Wie Schatten auf den Wogen schweben
Und schwinden wir,

Und messen unsre trägen Tritte
Nach Raum und Zeit;

Und sind (und wissens nicht) in Mitte
Der Ewigkeit.

A dream – 't is but a dream, our being
Here on this star.

On rolling waves a shadow fleeing
Is all we are.

By clock and rod we gauge our paces
And do not see

Staring at us – before our faces –
Eternity.

Alexander Gode

Gottfried August Bürger

LENORE

Lenore fuhr ums Morgenrot
empor aus schweren Träumen:
„Bist untreu, Wilhelm, oder tot?
Wie lange willst du säumen?" —
Er war mit König Friedrichs Macht
gezogen in die Prager Schlacht
und hatte nicht geschrieben,
ob er gesund geblieben.

Der König und die Kaiserin,
Des langen Haders müde,
Erweichten ihren harten Sinn
Und machten endlich Friede;
Und jedes Heer, mit Sing und Sang,
Mit Paukenschlag und Kling und Klang,
Geschmückt mit grünen Reisern,
Zog heim zu seinen Häusern.

Und überall, allüberall,
Auf Wegen und auf Stegen,
Zog alt und jung dem Jubelschall
Der Kommenden entgegen.
„Gottlob!" rief Kind und Gattin laut,
„Willkommen!" manche frohe Braut;
Ach! aber für Lenoren
War Gruß und Kuß verloren.

Sie frug den Zug wohl auf und ab
Und frug nach allen Namen;
Doch keiner war, der Kundschaft gab,

LENORE

Lenore awoke when skies were red,
Of grievous dreams complaining:
"Art faithless, William, now – or dead?
Too long away remaining!"
With Frederick King of Prussia's might
He'd marched to Prague to bravely fight.
The silence was unbroken.

The King and Austria's Empress too
Of quarreling were tired;
They pity on their people knew,
And both now peace desired;
The soldiers all sang merry songs,
With cornets, drums and clash of gongs,
With branches green so gaily
Came ever nearer daily.

And everywhere from everywhere
On roads and bypaths winding,
Both young and old came marching there,
Their dearly loved ones finding.
"Praise God!" both wives and children cried,
And "Welcome!" many a happy bride.
Lenore's belov'd was missing,
No greeting and no kissing.

She questioned here and questioned there,
For news of William seeking,
But none of those who present were

Von allen, so da kamen.
Als nun das Heer vorüber war,
Zerraufte sie das Rabenhaar
Und warf sich hin zur Erde
Mit wütiger Gebärde.

Die Mutter lief wohl hin zu ihr:
,,Ach, daß sich Gott erbarme!
Du trautes Kind, was ist mit dir?" –
Und schloß sie in die Arme –
,,O Mutter, Mutter, hin ist hin!
Nun fahre Welt und alles hin!
Bei Gott ist kein Erbarmen.
O weh, o weh mir Armen!" –

"Hilf Gott! hilf! Sieh uns gnädig an!
Kind, bet ein Vaterunser!
Was Gott tut, das ist wohlgetan,
Gott, Gott erbarmt sich unser!"
,,O Mutter! Mutter! eitler Wahn!
Gott hat an mir nicht wohlgetan!
Was half, was half mein Beten?
Nun ist's nicht mehr vonnöten."

,,Hilf, Gott, hilf! Wer den Vater kennt,
Der weiß, er hilft den Kindern.
Das hochgelobte Sakrament
Wird deinen Jammer lindern." –
,,O Mutter, Mutter, was mich brennt,
Das lindert mir kein Sakrament!
Kein Sakrament mag Leben
Den Toten wiedergeben." –

Of William could be speaking.
When now the host had marched away,
She tore her raven hair and lay
Upon the earth there moaning,
In rage and anger groaning.

But now her mother ran to see. . . .
"Oh God, do not forsake her!
My child, what has come over thee?"
Into her arms she takes her.
"Oh mother, mother, done is done!
I curse the world, the earth, the sun!
For God is me forsaking;
Alas, my poor heart's breaking!"

"Oh help us, God, and mercy show!
Child, pray for mercy on us!
Do not revile what God does so!
God will have pity on us."
"Oh mother, mother, all is vain!
God from me every hope has ta'en!
Of what avail my praying?
Is William with me staying?"

"The Father always help has sent,
His children's lot to brighten,
The high and holy sacrament
Thy grief and woe will lighten."
"Oh mother, flames that in me burn
No sacrament away will turn!
No sacrament can living
To those who died be giving."

„Hör, Kind! Wie, wenn der falsche Mann
Im fernen Ungarlande
Sich seines Glaubens abgetan
Zum neuen Ehebande?
Laß fahren, Kind, sein Herz dahin!
Er hat es nimmermehr Gewinn!
Wenn Seel' und Leib sich trennen,
Wird ihn sein Meineid brennen!" –

„O Mutter! Mutter! hin ist hin!
Verloren ist verloren!
Der Tod, der Tod ist mein Gewinn!
O wär ich nie geboren!
Lisch aus, mein Licht! auf ewig aus!
Stirb hin, stirb hin in Nacht und Graus!
Bei Gott ist kein Erbarmen;
O weh, o weh mir Armen!" –

„Hilf, Gott, hilf! Geh nicht ins Gericht
Mit deinem armen Kinde!
Sie weiß nicht, was die Zunge spricht;
Behalt ihr nicht die Sünde!
Ach, Kind, vergiß dein irdisch Leid,
Und denk an Gott und Seligkeit!
So wird doch deiner Seelen
Der Bräutigam nicht fehlen" –

„O Mutter! was ist Seligkeit?
O Mutter! was ist Hölle?
Bei ihm, bei ihm ist Seligkeit,
Und ohne Wilhelm Hölle! –
Lisch aus, mein Licht, auf ewig aus!
Stirb hin, stirb hin in Nacht und Graus!
Ohn' ihn mag ich auf Erden,
Mag dort nicht selig werden" –

"Perhaps this man, whom thou dost mourn,
His faith has now forsaken,
From Hungary will ne'er return,
And there a wife has taken.
Oh let him go, thy grieving cease,
He'll never know a moment's peace;
When soul from body's parting
His conscience will be smarting."

"Oh mother, mother, done is done!
And lost is gone forever!
For death, for death is all I've won,
Such life is welcome never.
Forever may my light go out!
And may it die in night and rout!
For God has me forsaken,
And all from me has taken."

"Oh Lord, judge not! On Thee I call,
Judge not thy child severely!
She knows not what she says at all,
'Tis grief and sorrow, merely.
Oh child, forget thy earthly woe,
And think of where thy soul must go;
In heaven, then, believe me,
A bridegroom will receive thee."

"Oh mother, what is Paradise?
Oh mother, what's damnation?
With him, with him is Paradise,
And where he's not . . . damnation.
Forever let my light go out!
And may it die in night and rout!
For me there are no pleasures
In earth's or heaven's treasures."

So wütete Verzweifelung
Ihr in Gehirn und Adern.
Sie fuhr mit Gottes Vorsehung
Vermessen fort zu hadern,
Zerschlug den Busen und zerrang
Die Hand bis Sonnenuntergang,
Bis auf am Himmelsbogen
Die goldnen Sterne zogen.

Und außen, horch! gings trapp trapp trapp
Als wie von Rosses Hufen,
Und klirrend stieg ein Reiter ab
An des Geländers Stufen.
Und horch! und horch den Pfortenring,
Ganz lose, leise, klinglingling!
Dann kamen durch die Pforte
Vernehmlich diese Worte:

,,Holla, holla! Tu auf, mein Kind!
Schläfst, Liebchen, oder wachst du?
Wie bist noch gegen mich gesinnt?
Und weinest oder lachst du?" –
,,Ach, Wilhelm, du? – So spät bei Nacht?
Geweinet hab ich und gewacht;
Ach! großes Leid erlitten!
Wo kommst du hergeritten?" –

,,Wir satteln nur um Mitternacht.
Weit ritt ich her von Böhmen:
Ich habe spät mich aufgemacht
und will dich mit mir nehmen!" –
,,Ach, Wilhelm, erst herein geschwind!
Den Hagedorn durchsaust der Wind,
herein, in meinen Armen,
Herzliebster, zu erwarmen!"

And so dark rage and black despair
Her mind and body harried;
Her quarrel with God's all-loving care
Presumptuously she carried.
She wrung her hands and beat her breast
Until the sun had gone to rest,
Until the heavens darkling
With golden stars were sparkling.

But hear! Outside, a clop clop clop!
The sound is ever clearer;
The rider comes to jingling stop,
His steps now bring him nearer.
Oh hear, oh hear the door-bell ring
And softly, softly ding ding ding!
He did not knock but merely
These words were heard quite clearly:

"Hello! Hello! The door, my child!
Art waking, love, or sleeping?
Art thou in anger now or mild,
Art laughing, or art weeping?"
"Oh William, William, can it be?
I've wept so much I scarce can see;
Oh sorrow's with me biding!
Oh, whence hast thou come riding?"

"At midnight thou and I shall ride,
Bohemia's where I started.
I've ridden quickly to thy side,
And we'll no more be parted."
"Oh William, come in quickly, do!
The wind the hawthorn rages through.
In here it is not storming,
Thy limbs I'll soon be warming."

„Laß sausen durch den Hagedorn,
laß sausen, Kind, laß sausen!
Der Rappe scharrt, es klirrt der Sporn;
ich darf allhier nicht hausen.
Komm, schürze, spring und schwinge dich
auf meinen Rappen hinter mich!
Muß heut noch hundert Meilen
mit dir ins Brautbett eilen." –

„Ach, wolltest hundert Meilen noch
mich heut ins Brautbett tragen?
Und horch, es brummt die Glocke noch,
die elf schon angeschlagen." –
„Sieh hin, sieh her, der Mond scheint hell;
wir und die Toten reiten schnell,
ich bringe dich, zur Wette,
noch heut ins Hochzeitbette." –

„Sag an, wo ist dein Kämmerlein?
Wo?, wie dein Hochzeitbettchen?" –
„Weit, weit von hier! Still, kühl und klein! –
Sechs Bretter und zwei Brettchen!" –
„Hat's Raum für mich?" – „Für dich und mich!
Komm, schürze, spring und schwinge dich!
Die Hochzeitsgäste hoffen!
Die Kammer steht uns offen." –

Schön Liebchen schürzte, sprang und schwang
sich auf das Roß behende;
wohl um den trauten Reiter schlang
sie ihre Lilienhände,
und hurre hurre, hopp hopp hopp!
Ging's fort in sausendem Galopp,
daß Roß und Reiter schnoben
und Kies und Funken stoben.

"Then let the wind howl through the hedge,
Let howl, lass, stronger, stronger!
The black horse paws, the spurs have edge,
I can't remain here longer.
Come dress and with a leap thou be
Upon the black horse here with me.
There's a hundred miles to cover
To joys of love and lover."

"A hundred miles must we away
Our bridal bed to sleep in?
Oh listen, night is on the way,
And here's a bed to creep in."
"See there! The moon shines clear and bright.
We and the dead ride fast tonight.
Midnight, I pledge will find us
The wedding rites behind us."

"Oh tell me, where's the little room,
The bed that I've a share of?"
"Far, far from here, cool silent tomb,
Six planks, small boards a pair of."
"There's room for me?" "For me and thee!
Come hurry, dress and ride with me.
The wedding guests are waiting,
Our nuptials celebrating."

She dressed herself, to horse she swung,
Onto the horse beside her;
Her soft white arms she straightway flung
Around the urgent rider.
And hurry, hurry, hop hop hop!
In reckless gallop, clop clop clop!
The snorting steed was speeding
Through stones and sparks unheeding.

Zur rechten und zur linken Hand,
Vorbei vor ihren Blicken,
Wie flogen Anger, Heid' und Land!
Wie donnerten die Brücken! –
„Graut Liebchen auch? – der Mond scheint hell!
Hurra! die Toten reiten schnell!
Graut Liebchen auch vor Toten?" –
„Ach nein! – Doch laß die Toten!" –

Was klang dort für Gesang und Klang?
Was flatterten die Raben? –
Horch Glockenklang! Horch Totensang:
„Laßt uns den Leib begraben!"
Und näher zog ein Leichenzug,
Der Sarg und Totenbahre trug.
Das Lied war zu vergleichen
Dem Unkenruf in Teichen.

„Nach Mitternacht begrabt den Leib
Mit Klang und Sang und Klage!
Jetzt führ ich heim mein junges Weib.
Mit, mit zum Brautgelage!
Komm, Küster, hier! komm mit dem Chor
Und gurgle mir das Brautlied vor!
Komm, Pfaff, und sprich den Segen.
Eh wir zu Bett uns legen!" –

Still Klang und Sang – die Bahre schwand.
Gehorsam seinem Rufen
Kams, hurre! hurre! nachgerannt
Hart hinters Rappen Hufen.
Und immer weiter, hopp hopp hopp!
Gings fort in sausendem Galopp,
Daß Roß und Reiter schnoben
Und Kies und Funken stoben.

As they rode on, on either hand
Before their eyes were flashing
The flying turf and heath and land,
And hoofs on bridges crashing.
"Art thou afraid? The moon shines bright!
Hurrah! the dead ride fast tonight!
Art thou afraid of dead men?"
"Let be, let be the dead men!"

What song rang out the road along?
And flutter here the ravens?
Hear! Clang of bells! Hear! Burial song!
"The dead to their last havens!"
A burial party nearer drew,
A bier and coffin bore the crew.
Their singing was appalling,
Like frogs in sedge-pools calling.

"Now dig the grave when midnight's past,
With clang and song and wailing;
With my young bride I'm riding fast,
Let not the feast be failing.
Come, sexton, here! Bring all along!
And gurgle out the bridal song.
Come, priest and speak the blessing.
'Tis late and time is pressing."

The bier falls back . . . still clang and song. . . .
His urgent call obeying,
And hurry, hurry, ran along
Behind the black horse staying.
And farther, farther, hop hop hop!
The black horse galloped, clop clop clop!
The snorting steed was speeding,
Through sparks and stones unheeding.

Wie flogen rechts, wie flogen links
Gebirge, Bäum' und Hecken!
Wie flogen links und rechts und links
Die Dörfer, Städt' und Flecken! –
„Graut Liebchen auch? – Der Mond scheint hell!
Hurra! die Toten reiten schnell!
Graut Liebchen auch vor Toten?" –
„Ach! laß sie ruhn, die Toten!" –

Sieh da! sieh da! Am Hochgericht
tanzt' um des Rades Spindel
halb sichtbarlich bei Mondenlicht
ein luftiges Gesindel.
„Sa! sa! Gesindel! hier! komm hier!
Gesindel, komm und folge mir!
Tanz uns den Hochzeitsreigen,
wenn wir zu Bette steigen!" –

Und das Gesindel husch husch husch!
Kam hinten nachgeprasselt,
wie Wirbelwind am Haselbusch
durch dürre Blätter rasselt.
Und weiter, weiter, hopp hopp hopp!
Ging's fort in sausendem Galopp,
daß Roß und Reiter schnoben
und Kies und Funken stoben.

Wie flog, was rund der Mond beschien,
Wie flog es in die Ferne!
Wie flogen oben überhin
Der Himmel und die Sterne! –
„Graut Liebchen auch? – der Mond scheint hell!
Hurra! die Toten reiten schnell!
Graut Liebchen auch vor Toten?" –
„O weh! laß ruhn die Toten!". . .

Now flew to right, now flew to left
The hedges, trees and mountains;
Now flew to left and right and left
Towns, cities, village fountains.
"Art thou afraid? The moon shines bright!
Hurrah! the dead ride fast tonight!
Art thou afraid of dead men?"
"Let rest, let rest the dead men!"

By scaffold high . . . a ghastly sight. . . .
Around a wheel there dancing,
Half visible in pale moonlight,
A ghostly crew is prancing.
"Hello, there! Devil's crew, come here!
Come, follow coffin and the bier!
For wedding dance we're yearning,
Our hearts for love are burning."

And that black crew then rush rush rush!
Came rattling on and hustling,
As whirlpool through a hazelbush
Goes through the dry leaves rustling.
And farther, farther, hop hop hop!
The black horse galloped, clop clop clop
The snorting steed was speeding
Through sparks and stones unheeding.

And all on which the pale moon shone
Soon far away was flying;
The sky and stars were likewise gone,
The rider madly crying:
"Art thou afraid? The moon shines bright!
Hurrah! the dead ride fast tonight!
Art thou afraid of dead men?"
"Woe's me, let rest the dead men!"

„Rapp'! Rapp'! Mich dünkt, der Hahn schon ruft . . .
bald wird der Sand verrinnen . . .
Rapp'! Rapp'! ich wittre Morgenluft . . .
Rapp'! tummle dich von hinnen!
Vollbracht, vollbracht ist unser Lauf!
Das Hochzeitbette tut sich auf!
Die Toten reiten schnelle!
Wir sind, wir sind zur Stelle." –

Rasch auf ein eisern Gittertor
ging's mit verhängtem Zügel;
mit schwanker Gert' ein Schlag davor
zersprengte Schloß und Riegel.
Die Flügel flogen klirrend auf,
und über Gräber ging der Lauf;
es blinkten Leichensteine
rundum im Mondenscheine.

Ha sieh! Ha sieh! Im Augenblick,
hu! hu! ein gräßlich Wunder!
Des Reiters Koller, Stück für Stück,
fiel ab wie mürber Zunder,
zum Schädel ohne Zopf und Schopf,
zum nackten Schädel ward sein Kopf,
sein Körper zum Gerippe
mit Stundenglas und Hippe.

Hoch bäumte sich, wild schnob der Rapp'
und sprühte Feuerfunken;
und hui! war's unter ihr hinab
verschwunden und versunken.
Geheul! Geheul aus hoher Luft,
Gewinsel kam aus tiefer Gruft.
Lenorens Herz mit Beben
rang zwischen Tod und Leben.

"Come, Black, methinks the cock now crows,
The sand is quickly draining.
Black! Black! The morning light now grows!
Black, hurry! Time is waning!
Our ride is finished, now is past,
We've reached the bridal bed at last.
Ah, how the dead ride madly!
The bed we welcome gladly."

The horse now went with pace full slow
To an iron gate, and wonder
Of wonders! soon a gentle blow
Tore lock and bolt asunder.
The gate with creaking opened wide,
And over graves they went inside,
The gravestones there all seeming
To glare in the moonlight gleaming.

But see! Will wonders never cease?
Oh horror misbegotten!
The rider's doublet piece by piece
Fell off like tinder rotten.
Without his hair his brain-pan there
Became a naked skull and bare,
His skeleton full mickle
With hour-glass and sickle.

The snorting horse reared up for flight,
Far sparks of fire sending,
And in a trice was gone from sight,
Into the depths descending.
And howling came from out the air,
And moaning from the black depths there.
Lenore's heart was abreaking,
For death its toll was taking.

Nun tanzten wohl bei Mondenglanz
rundum herum im Kreise
die Geister einen Kettentanz
und heulten diese Weise:
,,Geduld! Geduld! Wenn's Herz auch bricht!
Mit Gott im Himmel hadre nicht!
Des Leibes bist du ledig;
Gott sei der Seele gnädig!‘‘

And dancing, while the moon shone bright,
Their rounds of death and mourning,
The spirits sang from depth and height
In howling tones this warning:
"Resign! Resign! Though hearts may rend!
'Gainst God in Heaven do not fend!
Your life on earth has ended.
In God's grace be commended!"

Francis Owen

Ludwig Christoph Hölty

MAINACHT

Wenn der silberne Mond durch die Gesträuche blickt
Und sein schlummerndes Licht über den Rasen geußt
Und die Nachtigall flötet,
Wandl' ich traurig von Busch zu Busch.

Überhüllet von Laub, girret ein Taubenpaar
Sein Entzücken mir vor; aber ich wende mich;
Suche dunklere Schatten,
Und die einsame Träne rinnt.

Wann, o lächelndes Bild, welches wie Morgenrot
Durch die Seel mir strahlt, find' ich auf Erden dich?
Und die einsame Träne
Bebt mir heißer die Wang' herab!

NIGHT IN MAY

Now the silvery moon peeps through the arch of leaves,
Spilling its drowsy light over the walks and lawns,
And the nightingales carol.
Sad, I wander from bush to bush.

Hidden among the leaves, a turtledove and his mate
Coo their rapturous love, making me turn aside,
Seeking gloomier shadows.
And a desolate teardrop falls.

O, you sweet, smiling face, kindling within my heart
All the glory of dawn! Are you only a dream?
And the desolate teardrops,
Brimming over, roll down my cheek.

Helen Sebba

Leopold Friedrich Günther von Goeckingk

ALS DER ERSTE SCHNEE FIEL

Gleich einem König, der in seine Staaten
Zurück als Sieger kehrt, empfängt ein Jubel dich!
Der Knabe balgt um deine Flocken sich
Wie bei der Krönung um Dukaten.

Selbst mir, obschon ein Mädchen und der Rute
Lang nicht mehr untertan, bist du ein lieber Gast;
Denn siehst du nicht, seit du die Erde hast
So weich belegt, wie ich mich spute,

Zu fahren, ohne Segel, ohne Räder,
Auf einer Muschel hin durch deinen weißen Flor,
So sanft und doch so leicht, so schnell, wie vor
Dem Westwind eine Flaumenfeder.

Aus allen Fenstern und aus allen Türen
Sieht mir der bleiche Neid aus hohlen Augen nach;
Selbst die Matrone wird ein leises Ach
Und einen Wunsch um mich verlieren.

Denn der, um den wir Mädchen oft uns stritten,
Wird hinter mir, so schlank wie eine Tanne, stehn
Und sonst auf nichts mit seinen Augen sehn
Als auf das Mädchen in dem Schlitten.

AS THE FIRST SNOW FELL

Like to a monarch who in triumph takes
His way home through his lands, you hear our cheers resound!
And, as for ducats when a king is crowned,
The children battle for your flakes.

Although a maid and from the switch's sway
Long since released, e'en I think you a welcome guest;
Do you not see, since softly you have dressed
The ground, how I no more delay?

Set on a shell, with neither wheels nor sail,
I shall be borne across your meadowland of white
As easily and yet as swift and light
As down before the western gale.

From every window and from every gate
Pale envy will pursue me with her sunken eye;
Seeing me, even the matron lets a cry
Escape, and makes a wish its mate.

For he, who's often been our maiden prey,
Will stand behind me there, as slender as the spruce,
And watching naught else, his eye will not turn loose
The girl before him on the sleigh.

George C. Schoolfield

NACH DEM ERSTEN NÄCHTLICHEN BESUCHE

Bin ich nüchtern, bin ich trunken?
Wach ich oder träum ich nur?
Bin ich aus der Welt gesunken?
Bin ich anderer Natur?
Fühlt' ein Mädchen schon so was?
Wie begreif ich alles das?

Weiß ich, daß die Rosen blühen?
Hör ich jene Raben schrein?
Fühl ich, wie die Wangen glühen?
Schmeck ich einen Tropfen Wein?
Seh ich dieses Morgenrot? –
Tot sind alle Sinnen, tot!

Alle seid ihr denn gestillet?
Alle? Habet alle Dank!
Könnt ich so in mich gehüllet,
Ohne Speis und ohne Trank,
Nur so sitzen Tag für Tag
Bis zum letzten Herzensschlag.

In die Nacht der Freude fliehet
Meine Seele wieder hin!
Hört und schmeckt und fühlt und siehet
Mit dem feinen innren Sinn;
O Gedächtnis! schon in dir
Liegt ein ganzer Himmel mir.

Worte, wie sie abgerissen
Kaum ein Seufzer von ihm stieß,
Hör ich wieder, fühl ihn küssen:

AFTER THE FIRST NOCTURNAL VISIT

Am I sober now or drunk?
Do I wake or only dream?
Have I from creation sunk?
Am I other than I seem?
Suit such feelings maidenhood?
How can they be understood?

Do I know the blooming rose?
Do I hear the raven's cry?
Do I feel how my cheek glows?
Does at wine my taste go dry?
Do I see the dawn turn red?
Dead are all my senses, dead.

Have you all been satisfied?
Take my thanks, if thus you think!
Could I but within me bide
Without food and without drink,
Sit day in, day out apart
'Til the last beat of my heart.

To the night of pleasure flees
Once again my spirit hence,
Hears and tastes and feels and sees
With its keen and inner sense;
Even in you, memory,
Lies a heaven all for me.

All those stuttered words that miss
Meaning, I hear him repeat,
Scarce sighed out – I feel his kiss:

Welche Sprache sagt, wie süß?
Seh ein Tränchen – komm herab!
Meine Lippe küßt dich ab!

Wie ich noch so vor ihm stehe,
Immer spreche: gute Nacht!
Bald ihn stockend wieder flehe:
Bleibe, bis der Hahn erwacht!
Wie mein Fuß bei jedem Schritt
Wanket, und mein Liebster mit.

Wie ich nun, an seine Seite
Festgeklammert, küssend ihn
Durch den Garten hin begleite,
Bald uns halten, bald uns ziehn!
Wie da Mond und Sterne stehn,
Unserm Abschied zuzusehn.

Ach, da sind wir an der Türe!
Bebend hält er in der Hand
Schon den Schlüssel. – Wart, ich spüre
Jemand gehen, Amarant!
Warte nur das bißchen doch!
Einen Kuß zum Abschied noch!

Ich verliere, ich verliere
Mich in diesem Labyrinth!
Träumt ich je, dass ich erführe,
Was für Freuden Freuden sind?
Wenn die Freude töten kann,
Triffst du nie mich wieder an.

Tongue can never tell how sweet!
There's a teardrop – come, descend!
Lips will bring your fall to end!

Now I hold him at arm's reach,
Whispering: "Good night, good night!"
Now I stop and but beseech
Him to stay 'til cock greets light.
My foot, at every move anew,
Falters, and my lover too.

And I see how at his side –
Stopping now, now passing on,
Kissing him – I am his guide,
Tightly nestled, down the lawn,
While the moon and stars convene,
Gazing at our farewell scene.

Oh, now we are at the gate:
Trembling hands are forced to try
The key within the lock. But wait,
Amarant, someone goes by.
Wait for but a moment more!
Take a last kiss at the door!

In this labyrinth I go,
In this maze-way losing me!
Did I dream that I should know
Just how joyful joys can be?
Why, if joy can cause our death,
I have drawn my dying breath.

George C. Schoolfield

Johann Wolfgang Goethe

DAS VEILCHEN

Ein Veilchen auf der Wiese stand,
Gebückt in sich und unbekannt;
Es war ein herzigs Veilchen.
Da kam eine junge Schäferin
Mit leichtem Schritt und munterm Sinn
Daher, daher,
Die Wiese her, und sang.

Ach! denkt das Veilchen, wär' ich nur
Die schönste Blume der Natur,
Ach, nur ein kleines Weilchen,
Bis mich das Liebchen abgepflückt
Und an dem Busen matt gedrückt!
Ach nur, ach nur
Ein Viertelstündchen lang!

Ach! aber ach! das Mädchen kam
Und nicht in acht das Veilchen nahm,
Ertrat das arme Veilchen.
Es sank und starb und freut' sich noch:
Und sterb' ich denn, so sterb' ich doch
Durch sie, durch sie,
Zu ihren Füßen doch.

THE VIOLET

A violet on the lea had grown,
Stood lowly bent and unbeknown;
It was a lovely violet.
Then came a sweet young shepherdess
Of blithesome step and mood to bless
Along, along,
Along the lea and sang.

Ah! thought the violet, could I be
The prettiest flower upon the lea
For just a little while yet,
Until my truelove gathers me
And on her bosom smothers me,
O just, o just
A little moment more.

Alack the day! The maid passed by
And to the violet turned no eye,
Trod on the dainty violet.
It sank and died and still was glad:
Be this the end, the end I've had
Through her, through her,
And at my truelove's feet.

Alexander Gode

HEIDENRÖSLEIN

Sah ein Knab' ein Röslein stehn,
Röslein auf der Heiden,
War so jung und morgenschön,
Lief er schnell, es nah zu sehn,
Sah's mit vielen Freuden.
Röslein, Röslein, Röslein rot,
Röslein auf der Heiden.

Knabe sprach: „Ich breche dich,
Röslein auf der Heiden!"
Röslein sprach: „Ich steche dich,
Daß du ewig denkst an mich,
Und ich will's nicht leiden."
Röslein, Röslein, Röslein rot,
Röslein auf der Heiden.

Und der wilde Knabe brach
's Röslein auf der Heiden;
Röslein wehrte sich und stach,
Half ihm doch kein Weh und Ach,
Mußt' es eben leiden.
Röslein, Röslein, Röslein rot,
Röslein auf der Heiden.

ROSE AMID THE HEATHER

Saw a lad a rose one day,
Rose amid the heather,
'Twas so fresh and morning-fair
Quick he ran to see it there,
Saw it with much pleasure.
Rose, O rose, O rose so red,
Rose amid the heather.

Said the lad, "I'll pick thee then,
Rose amid the heather!"
Said the rose, "I'll prick thee then,
So thou'lt think of me again,
And I'll bear it never."
Rose, O rose, O rose so red,
Rose amid the heather.

And the wild young laddie picked
Rose amid the heather;
Rose resisted then and pricked,
Crying "Woe!" helped not a bit,
Had to bear it ever.
Rose, O rose, O rose so red,
Rose amid the heather.

Lynda A. Marvin

AN LIDA

Den einzigen, Lida, welchen du lieben kannst,
Forderst du ganz für dich und mit Recht.
Auch ist er einzig dein,
Denn seit ich von dir bin,
Scheint mir des schnellsten Lebens
Lärmende Bewegung
Nur ein leichter Flor, durch den ich deine Gestalt
Immerfort wie in Wolken erblicke:
Sie leuchtet mir freundlich und treu,
Wie durch des Nordlichts bewegliche Strahlen
Ewige Sterne schwimmen.

TO LIDA

The only one, Lida, whom you can love
You claim wholly for your own, and rightly.
And he, too, is wholly yours.
Since absent from you
In life's turmoils, I see nothing
But a floating mist through which
Forever I discern your form
As though in clouds:
Friendly and true it shines for me
As through the far-flickering rays of northern lights
Glimmer eternal stars.

Philip Allan Friedman

Ach, um deine feuchten Schwingen,
West, wie sehr ich dich beneide:
Denn du kannst ihm Kunde bringen,
Was ich in der Trennung leide!

Die Bewegung deiner Flügel
Weckt im Busen stilles Sehnen;
Blumen, Augen, Wald und Hügel
Stehn bei deinem Hauch in Tränen.

Doch dein mildes, sanftes Wehen
Kühlt die wunden Augenlider;
Ach, für Leid müßt' ich vergehen,
Hofft ich nicht zu sehn ihn wieder.

Eile denn zu meinem Lieben,
Spreche sanft zu seinem Herzen;
Doch vermeid, ihn zu betrüben,
Und verbirg ihm meine Schmerzen.

Sag ihm, aber sags bescheiden,
Seine Liebe sei mein Leben;
Freudiges Gefühl von beiden
Wird mir seine Nähe geben.

Ah, your dewy pinions swinging
Eastward, West-wind I would borrow,
For I know that swiftly winging
You can tell him how I sorrow.

Here your swaying wings, oh Blower,
Wake a longing unresisted;
Eye and tree and hill and flower
At your breath in tears are misted.

Yet your wafting, mild and tender,
Cools the eyelids of their burning;
Ah, to grief I should surrender,
But for hope of his returning.

Then to my beloved hasten;
Whisper to his heart; but bidden
To forbear to grieve or chasten,
Wind, my pain from him keep hidden.

Tell, in manner unassuming,
My life is his love unshaken,
And of both a joyous blooming
Will his nearness for me waken.

Aurelia G. Scott

NÄHE DES GELIEBTEN

Ich denke dein, wenn mir der Sonne Schimmer
    Vom Meere strahlt;
Ich denke dein, wenn sich des Mondes Flimmer
    In Quellen malt.

Ich sehe dich, wenn auf dem fernen Wege
    Der Staub sich hebt;
In tiefer Nacht, wenn auf dem schmalen Stege
    Der Wand'rer bebt.

Ich höre dich, wenn dort mit dumpfem Rauschen
    Die Welle steigt;
Im stillen Haine geh' ich oft zu lauschen,
    Wenn alles schweigt.

Ich bin bei dir, du seist auch noch so ferne,
    Du bist mir nah!
Die Sonne sinkt, bald leuchten mir die Sterne.
    O, wärst du da!

MY LOVE IS NEAR

I think of thee when from the ocean glimmer
The sun's bright beams;
I think of thee when in the streamlets shimmer
The moon's pale gleams.

I see thy form when on the distant highway
The dust cloud plays;
In deep dark night when on the narrow byway
The wanderer sways.

I hear thy voice when waves with low deep swelling
To shoreward spill;
In silent groves I hear thy voice compelling,
When all is still.

Though far away thou'rt with me in my dreaming,
Thou art so near!
The sun goes down and soon the stars are gleaming.
Oh, wert thou here!

Francis Owen

NACHTGEDANKEN

Euch bedaur ich, unglückselige Sterne,
Die ihr schön seid und so herrlich scheinet,
Dem bedrängten Schiffer gerne leuchtet,
Unbelohnt von Göttern und von Menschen:
Denn ihr liebt nicht, kanntet nie die Liebe!
Unaufhaltsam führen ewige Stunden
Eure Reihen durch den weiten Himmel.
Welche Reise habt ihr schon vollendet,
Seit ich weilend in dem Arm der Liebsten
Euer und der Mitternacht vergessen.

NIGHT THOUGHTS

Stars, I pity you and call you hapless!
Ye are beautiful, ye shine in splendor,
Gladly light the way for hard-pressed sailors,
Yet by gods and men are unrewarded:
For ye love not, have of love no knowledge!
Sojournless, eternal hours lead you,
Countless hosts, through infinite expanses.
Think, what journey have ye not accomplished!
While I, ling'ring in my love's embraces,
Thought of neither you nor midnight's passing.

Alexander Gode

HARFENSPIELER

Wer nie sein Brot mit Tränen aß,
Wer nie die kummervollen Nächte
Auf seinem Bette weinend saß,
Der kennt euch nicht, ihr himmlischen Mächte!

Ihr führt ins Leben uns hinein,
Ihr laßt den Armen schuldig werden,
Dann überlaßt ihr ihn der Pein –
Denn alle Schuld rächt sich auf Erden.

SONG OF THE HARP-PLAYER

Who never ate his bread in tears,
Who never sat the night's grim hours,
Weeping, upon his bed in fears,
He knows you not, ye Heavenly Powers!

You lead us into life's broad plain,
Let each live out his guilty birth,
Then give him over to his pain;
For all guilt is avenged on earth.

Herman Salinger

SELIGE SEHNSUCHT

Sagt es niemand, nur den Weisen,
Weil die Menge gleich verhöhnet;
Das Lebendge will ich preisen,
Das nach Flammentod sich sehnet.

In der Liebesnächte Kühlung,
Die dich zeugte, wo du zeugtest,
Überfällt dich fremde Fühlung,
Wenn die stille Kerze leuchtet.

Nicht mehr bleibest du umfangen
In der Finsternis Beschattung,
Und dich reißet neu Verlangen
Auf zu höherer Begattung.

Keine Ferne macht dich schwierig,
Kommst geflogen und gebannt,
Und zuletzt, des Lichts begierig,
Bist du Schmetterling verbrannt.

Und solang du das nicht hast,
Dieses: Stirb und werde!
Bist du nur ein trüber Gast
Auf der dunklen Erde.

BLISSFUL LONGING

Tell it no one but the wise,
Lest the many laugh in scorn:
Only such life can I prize
As through fire is reborn.

In the love-lists, deep nights through,
Giving, taking life in turn,
Alien feeling seizes you
While the tranquil tapers burn.

Then no more may you remain
Caught in this devouring fire,
But are driven forth again
Toward a nobler heart's-desire.

Never hindrance hindered yet,
You come flying through the night,
Eager night-moth, your heart set
On the new devouring light.

And till you have stood this test:
"Die, and come to birth!"
You remain a sorry guest
On this gloomy earth.

Albert Bloch

GANYMED

Wie im Morgenglanze
Du rings mich anglühst,
Frühling, Geliebter!
Mit tausendfacher Liebeswonne
Sich an mein Herz drängt
Deiner ewigen Wärme
Heilig Gefühl,
Unendliche Schöne!

Daß ich dich fassen möcht'
In diesen Arm!

Ach, an deinem Busen
Lieg ich, schmachte,
Und deine Blumen, dein Gras
Drängen sich an mein Herz.
Du kühlst den brennenden
Durst meines Busens,
Lieblicher Morgenwind!
Ruft drein die Nachtigall
Liebend nach mir aus dem Nebeltal.

Ich komm, ich komme!
Wohin? Ach, wohin?

Hinauf! Hinauf strebt's.
Es schweben die Wolken
Abwärts, die Wolken
Neigen sich der sehnenden Liebe.
Mir! Mir!

GANYMED

How you burn about me
As in the glow of morning,
Spring, my darling!
With thousandfold ecstasy of love
Pierces to my heart
The holy bliss
Of your eternal warmth,
O infinite beauty!

Oh, that I might clasp you
Within my arms!

Oh, on your bosom
I lie, I languish.
And your blossoms, your grass
Press against my heart.
You cool the burning
Thirst of my breast,
Beloved morning breeze!
The nightingale summons me
Lovingly from the misty valley.

I am coming, I am coming!
Where, oh, where?

Upwards! Upwards is the striving.
The clouds are sweeping
Downward, the clouds are
Bending to meet my yearning love.
To me! To me!

In euerm Schoße
Aufwärts!
Umfangend umfangen!
Aufwärts an deinen Busen,
All-liebender Vater!

In your lap,
Upwards!
Embracing, embraced!
Upwards to your bosom,
All-loving Father!

W. Edward Brown

GESANG DER GEISTER ÜBER DEN WASSERN

Des Menschen Seele
Gleicht dem Wasser:
Vom Himmel kommt es,
Zum Himmel steigt es,
Und wieder nieder
Zur Erde muß es,
Ewig wechselnd.

Strömt von der hohen,
Steilen Felswand
Der reine Strahl,
Dann stäubt er lieblich
In Wolkenwellen
Zum glatten Fels,
Und leicht empfangen
Wallt er verschleiernd,
Leisrauschend,
Zur Tiefe nieder.

Ragen Klippen
Dem Sturz entgegen,
Schäumt er unmutig
Stufenweise
Zum Abgrund.

Im flachen Bette
Schleicht er das Wiesental hin,
Und in dem glatten See
Weiden ihr Antlitz
Alle Gestirne.

SONG OF THE SPIRITS OVER THE WATERS

Man's soul
Is like the water:
From heaven descendeth it,
To heaven it riseth,
And down again
To earth it returneth,
Ever repeating.

When rushing headlong
From craggy sheer cliffs
Limpid the current falls,
Vapors rise softly,
Gracefully weaving
Over the barren rock,
Find friendly reception,
Sink, gentle deception,
Murmuring, swirling
Into the depth.

Stones thwart
Its progress,
Brimming ill-humor,
Haltingly floats it
To the abyss.

Caught in the shallows,
Crawls through the valleys;
Unruffled the lake
Mirrors the glory
Of heaven above.

Wind ist der Welle
Lieblicher Buhler;
Wind mischt von Grund aus
Schäumende Wogen.

Seele des Menschen,
Wie gleichst du dem Wasser!
Schicksal des Menschen,
Wie gleichst du dem Wind!

Wind is the lover,
Wave is the bride,
Wind tosses madly
Billows on high.

Soul of man,
Thou art as water,
Fate of man,
Thou art as wind.

R. L. Kahn

LIED DER PARZEN

Es fürchte die Götter
Das Menschengeschlecht!
Sie halten die Herrschaft
In ewigen Händen
Und können sie brauchen,
Wie's ihnen gefällt.

Der fürchte sie doppelt,
Den je sie erheben!
Auf Klippen und Wolken
Sind Stühle bereitet
Um goldene Tische.

Erhebet ein Zwist sich –
So stürzen die Gäste,
Geschmäht und geschändet,
In nächtliche Tiefen,
Und harren vergebens,
Im Finstern gebunden,
Gerechten Gerichtes.

Sie aber, sie bleiben
In ewigen Festen
An goldenen Tischen.
Sie schreiten vom Berge
Zu Bergen hinüber –
Aus Schlünden der Tiefe
Dampft ihnen der Atem
Erstickter Titanen,
Gleich Opfergerüchen,
Ein leichtes Gewölke.

SONG OF THE PARCAE

In fear of the gods let
The race of man stand!
Dominion they hold
In hands everlasting,
With power to use it
As they may see fit.

One whom they exalt
Should fear them twice over.
On cliffs and on clouds
Are chairs set out ready
At tables of gold.

If discord arises,
The guests may be cast,
Abused and dishonored,
To the depths of the dark
And there wait in vain,
Amid gloom and in fetters,
For judgment with justice.

Those others, however,
Sit endlessly feasting
At tables of gold.
And striding from mountain
Across to mountain,
They scent from the chasms
The smoking breath
Of the stifling Titans
Like a thin cloud of odor
Up-wafting from sacrifice.

Es wenden die Herrscher
Ihr segnendes Auge
Von ganzen Geschlechtern
Und meiden, im Enkel
Die ehmals geliebten
Still redenden Züge
Des Ahnherrn zu sehn.

So sangen die Parzen.
Es horcht der Verbannte
In nächtlichen Höhlen,
Der Alte, die Lieder,
Denkt Kinder und Enkel
Und schüttelt das Haupt.

These rulers avert
The eyes of their blessing
From whole generations,
Declining to see
In the grandson the grandsire's
Once well-beloved features
Now mute but eloquent.

So sang the Parcae.
The old one, the exile,
He harkens in hollows
Of night to these songs,
Thinks children and grandchildren,
And shakes his head.

Charles E. Passage

Natur und Kunst, sie scheinen sich zu fliehen
Und haben sich, eh man es denkt, gefunden;
Der Widerwille ist auch mir verschwunden,
Und beide scheinen gleich mich anzuziehen.

Es gilt wohl nur ein redliches Bemühen!
Und wenn wir erst in abgemeßnen Stunden
Mit Geist und Fleiß uns an die Kunst gebunden,
Mag frei Natur im Herzen wieder glühen.

So ists mit aller Bildung auch beschaffen.
Vergebens werden ungebundne Geister
Nach der Vollendung reiner Höhe streben.

Wer Großes will, muß sich zusammenraffen.
In der Beschränkung zeigt sich erst der Meister,
Und das Gesetz nur kann uns Freiheit geben.

Nature, it seems, must always clash with Art,
And yet, before we know it, both are one;
I too have learnt: their enmity is none,
Since each compels me, and in equal part.

Hard, honest work counts most! And once we start
To measure out the hours and never shun
Art's daily labor till our task is done,
Nature once more freely may move the heart.

So too all growth and ripening of the mind:
To the pure heights of ultimate consummation
In vain the unbound spirit seeks to flee.

Who seeks great gain leaves easy gain behind.
None proves a master but by limitation
And only law can give us liberty.

Michael Hamburger

DIE BRAUT VON KORINTH

Nach Korinthus von Athen gezogen
Kam ein Jüngling, dort noch unbekannt.
Einen Bürger hofft' er sich gewogen:
Beide Väter waren gastverwandt,
    Hatten frühe schon
    Töchterchen und Sohn
Braut und Bräutigam voraus genannt.

Aber wird er auch willkommen scheinen,
Wenn er teuer nicht die Gunst erkauft?
Er ist noch ein Heide mit den Seinen,
Und sie sind schon Christen und getauft.
    Keimt ein Glaube neu,
    Wird oft Lieb und Treu
Wie ein böses Unkraut ausgerauft.

Und schon lag das ganze Haus im stillen,
Vater, Töchter, nur die Mutter wacht;
Sie empfängt den Gast mit bestem Willen,
Gleich ins Prunkgemach wird er gebracht.
    Wein und Essen prangt,
    Eh er es verlangt:
So versorgend wünscht sie gute Nacht.

Aber bei dem wohlbestellten Essen
Wird die Lust der Speise nicht erregt.
Müdigkeit läßt Speis und Trank vergessen,
Daß er angekleidet sich aufs Bette legt;
    Und er schlummert fast,
    Als ein seltner Gast
Sich zur offnen Tür hereinbewegt.

THE BRIDE OF CORINTH

To Corinthus came, from Athens hailing,
Once a youth who, there unknown to most,
Hoped that townsman's aid would not be failing,
Who had been his father's guest and host.
At an early stage
When of tender age
Were the children pledgéd in a toast.

Will his welcome be with hesitations
If he cannot buy their favor prized?
He is pagan still, like his relations,
They are Christians, recently baptized.
When a creed is born,
Love and faith are torn
Often from the heart, like weeds despised.

Father, daughters, all the house is sleeping,
But the mother's lamp is still alight;
She receives the youth with friendly greeting,
To the guest room he is led forthright.
Food and wine are brought,
Even ere he thought;
All provided for, she bids good night.

But his taste for food is not excited,
Though a well-appointed meal is spread;
Food and drink by weariness are slighted,
Clothed he stretches out upon the bed;
But from sleep is wrest'
When so strange a guest
Enters through the door with silent tread.

Denn er sieht, bei seiner Lampe Schimmer
Tritt, mit weißem Schleier und Gewand,
Sittsam still ein Mädchen in das Zimmer,
Um die Stirn ein schwarz- und goldnes Band.
   Wie sie ihn erblickt,
   Hebt sie, die erschrickt,
Mit Erstaunen eine weiße Hand.

„Bin ich", rief sie aus, „so fremd im Hause,
Daß ich von dem Gaste nichts vernahm?
Ach, so hält man mich in meiner Klause!
Und nun überfällt mich hier die Scham.
   Ruhe nur so fort
   Auf dem Lager dort,
Und ich gehe schnell, so wie ich kam."

„Bleibe, schönes Mädchen!", ruft der Knabe,
Rafft von seinem Lager sich geschwind:
„Hier ist Ceres', hier ist Bacchus' Gabe,
Und du bringst den Amor, liebes Kind!
   Bist vor Schrecken blaß!
   Liebe, komm und laß,
Laß uns sehn, wie froh die Götter sind!"

„Ferne bleib, o Jüngling, bleibe stehen!
Ich gehöre nicht den Freuden an.
Schon der letzte Schritt ist, ach, geschehen
Durch der guten Mutter kranken Wahn,
   Die genesend schwur:
   Jugend und Natur
Sei dem Himmel künftig untertan.

In the glimmer that his lamp is throwing
Stands revealed a maid, demurely bland,
White her veil and white her garments flowing,
Round her head a black and golden band.
At his sudden sight,
She lifts up with fright
And astonishment a snow-white hand.

"Am I here a stranger, guests are bidden
To this house and I ignore their name?
Ah, they keep me in my cell, well hidden!
Here I stand now, overcome with shame.
To resume thy rest
On this couch is best,
And I leave as quickly as I came."

"Fairest maiden! Canst thou stay?" he queries.
From the couch he rises speedily;
"Here is Bacchus' gift and here is Ceres',
Amor, dearest child, is brought by thee!
Pale thou art, upset,
Dearest, come and let,
Let us see how glad the gods can be!"

"Stay away, O youth, by luck forsaken,
For the joys of life I am unfit.
Ah, the final step, it has been taken
By my ailing mother's clouded wit,
Who recov'ring vowed:
Nature should be cowed,
Youth, in future, must to heav'n submit.

Und der alten Götter bunt Gewimmel
Hat sogleich das stille Haus geleert.
Unsichtbar wird einer nur im Himmel,
Und ein Heiland wird am Kreuz verehrt;
   Opfer fallen hier,
   Weder Lamm noch Stier,
Aber Menschenopfer unerhört.‘‘

Und er fragt und wäget alle Worte,
Deren keines seinem Geist entgeht:
,,Ist es möglich, daß am stillen Orte
Die geliebte Braut hier vor mir steht?
   Sei die meine nur!
   Unsrer Väter Schwur
Hat vom Himmel Segen uns erfleht.‘‘

,,Mich erhältst du nicht, du gute Seele!
Meiner zweiten Schwester gönnt man dich.
Wenn ich mich in stiller Klause quäle,
Ach, in ihren Armen denk an mich,
   Die an dich nur denkt,
   Die sich liebend kränkt;
In die Erde bald verbirgt sie sich.‘‘

,,Nein, bei dieser Flamme seis geschworen,
Gütig zeigt sie Hymen uns voraus:
Bist der Freude nicht und mir verloren,
Kommst mit mir in meines Vaters Haus.
   Liebchen, bleibe hier!
   Feire gleich mit mir
Unerwartet unsern Hochzeitsschmaus!‘‘

"Of the ancient gods, in gay profusion,
Voided was the house for evermore.
One unseen, in heavenly seclusion,
On the cross, a saviour, they adore;
Sacrificed are here,
Neither lamb nor steer,
But the human victims by the score."

Then he asks and weighs what she is saying.
Not a word escapes his mind intent:
"Could it be that here I am surveying
Her, who for my dearest bride was meant?
Shouldst be mine anow!
For our fathers' vow
Grants us heaven's blessing and assent."

"Thou, my love, wilt not obtain me, never!
For my sister they have destined thee.
In my silent cell I pine forever,
Ah, when in her arms, remember me,
Whom thy sight does thrill,
Who for love is ill,
In the earth she soon will hidden be."

"No! and by this flame that Hymen lighted
Kindly in advance for us, I swear:
Art not lost to joy or me; united
To my father's house we shall repair.
Stay with me, my dear!
Unexpected here
We may celebrate our wedding fare!"

Und schon wechseln sie der Treue Zeichen:
Golden reicht sie ihm die Kette dar,
Und er will ihr eine Schale reichen,
Silbern, künstlich, wie nicht eine war.
    „Die ist nicht für mich;
    Doch, ich bitte dich,
Eine Locke gib von deinem Haar."

Eben schlug die dumpfe Geisterstunde,
Und nun schien es ihr erst wohl zu sein.
Gierig schlürfte sie mit blassem Munde
Nun den dunkel blutgefärbten Wein;
    Doch vom Weizenbrot,
    Das er freundlich bot,
Nahm sie nicht den kleinsten Bissen ein.

Und dem Jüngling reichte sie die Schale,
Der, wie sie, nun hastig lüstern trank.
Liebe fordert er beim stillen Mahle:
Ach, sein armes Herz war liebekrank!
    Doch sie widersteht,
    Wie er immer fleht,
Bis er weinend auf das Bette sank.

Und sie kommt und wirft sich zu ihm nieder:
„Ach, wie ungern seh ich dich gequält!
Aber, ach, berührst du meine Glieder,
Fühlst du schaudernd, was ich dir verhehlt.
    Wie der Schnee so weiß,
    Aber kalt wie Eis
Ist das Liebchen, das du dir erwählt."

Pledges of their troth ere long they offer;
She gives him a golden chain to wear,
He presents her with a precious coffer,
Wrought in silver and without compare.
"This is not for me;
But I beg of thee,
Let me have a ringlet of thy hair."

Midnight struck, the hour when ghosts are slinking,
Only now she seemed released from strain.
Pale-mouthed, avidly she started drinking
Wine, as dark and red as blood would stain;
Of the wheaten bread,
Though he gently pled,
E'en the smallest piece she did disdain.

To the youth she then a goblet proffered,
Who like her, with haste and relish drank.
Love he begged from her and love he offered;
"Ah, his love-sick heart was simple frank!
But she does not cede,
Though his passions plead,
Till he weeping on the pillows sank.

Then she throws herself beside him, kneeling:
"Ah! I hate the tortures I impose!
Should'st thou touch me though, thou wouldst be feeling
Shudd'ringly, what I must now disclose.
Marble-white of hue,
Cold as marble too
Is the maiden whom for love thou chose."

Heftig faßt er sie mit starken Armen,
Von der Liebe Jugendkraft durchmannt:
„Hoffe doch bei mir noch zu erwarmen,
Wärst du selbst mir aus dem Grab gesandt!"
 Wechselhauch und Kuß!
 Liebesüberfluß!
„Brennst du nicht und fühlest mich entbrannt?"

Liebe schließet fester sie zusammen,
Tränen mischen sich in ihre Lust;
Gierig saugt sie seines Mundes Flammen,
Eins ist nur im andern sich bewußt.
 Seine Liebeswut
 Wärmt ihr starres Blut,
Doch es schlägt kein Herz in ihrer Brust.

Unterdessen schleichet auf dem Gange
Häuslich spät die Mutter noch vorbei,
Horchet an der Tür und horchet lange,
Welch ein sonderbarer Ton es sei:
 Klag- und Wonnelaut,
 Bräutigams und Braut,
Und des Liebesstammelns Raserei!

Unbeweglich bleibt sie an der Türe,
Weil sie erst sich überzeugen muß,
Und sie hört die höchsten Liebesschwüre,
Lieb- und Schmeichelworte, mit Verdruß:
 „Still! der Hahn erwacht!" –
 „Aber morgen nacht
Bist du wieder da?" – und Kuß auf Kuß.

Strong of arm, he grasps her passionately,
Love's young power fills his manly frame:
"Hope thou still! My nearness warms thee greatly,
Wert thou even one the grave could claim!"
Breath-exchange and kiss,
Love's excess and bliss!
"Art thou burning, canst thou feel my flame?"

Love is binding them and strong desire,
Tears are mingling with their ecstasies;
Ardently she drinks his breath of fire,
Each one sentient through the other's bliss.
Though his frenzy could
Warm her frozen blood,
In her breast, no heartbeat answers his.

On her nightly round, from somewhere yonder,
Steals the mother through the gallery,
Listens at the door with growing wonder,
What this odd, mysterious sound might be:
Bride and groom the twain,
Voicing joy and pain,
Stammering with love-crazed urgency.

Stealthily about the door she hovers,
Making sure that something is amiss,
Vexed, she hears the greatest oaths of lovers,
Words of coaxing, words of love and bliss.
"Hark the cock crows – light!
But tomorrow night
Wilt thou come again?" – and kiss on kiss.

Länger hält die Mutter nicht das Zürnen,
Öffnet das bekannte Schloß geschwind:
„Gibt es hier im Hause solche Dirnen,
Die dem Fremden gleich zu Willen sind?"
　　So zur Tür hinein.
　　Bei der Lampe Schein
Sieht sie – Gott!, sie sieht ihr eigen Kind.

Und der Jüngling will im ersten Schrecken
Mit des Mädchens eignem Schleierflor,
Mit dem Teppich die Geliebte decken,
Doch sie windet gleich sich selbst hervor.
　　Wie mit Geists Gewalt
　　Hebet die Gestalt
Lang und langsam sich im Bett empor.

„Mutter! Mutter!", spricht sie hohle Worte,
„So mißgönnt Ihr mir die schöne Nacht!
Ihr vertreibt mich von dem warmen Orte,
Bin ich zur Verzweiflung nur erwacht?
　　Ists Euch nicht genug,
　　Daß ins Leichentuch,
Daß Ihr früh mich in das Grab gebracht?

Aber aus der schwerbedeckten Enge
Treibet mich ein eigenes Gericht.
Eurer Priester summende Gesänge
Und ihr Segen haben kein Gewicht;
　　Salz und Wasser kühlt
　　Nicht, wo Jugend fühlt;
Ach, die Erde kühlt die Liebe nicht!

But the mother, past endurance, wrenches
Ope the lock familiar to her.
"Does this building shelter whoring wenches,
Ready every stranger's bed to share?"
Enters thus the room,
In the lamplight's gloom
Sees, oh God! she sees her daughter there.

In his sudden fright, the youthful lover
Tries the flimsy veil the maid has shed,
Tries the carpet for his love as cover,
She unwinds, at once, what he has spread.
As with ghostly might,
To her fullest height,
Slowly she lifts up her form in bed.

"Mother," says she – hollow sounds her chiding –
"Thou dost grudge a night beside my groom!
Thou dost drive me from this cosy biding,
Have I wakened only to my doom?
Not enough thou vowed
Me into the shroud,
And so soon hast brought me to the tomb?

"But by higher judgment I am driven
From my heavy-lidded, narrow berth.
And the sing-song of thy priests has given
No relief; their blessing has no worth;
Salt and water soothe
Not the zest of youth;
Ah, love's ardor is not cooled by earth!

Dieser Jüngling war mir erst versprochen,
Als noch Venus' heitrer Tempel stand.
Mutter, habt Ihr doch das Wort gebrochen,
Weil ein fremd, ein falsch Gelübd' Euch band!
   Doch kein Gott erhört,
   Wenn die Mutter schwört,
Zu versagen ihrer Tochter Hand.

Aus dem Grabe werd ich ausgetrieben,
Noch zu suchen das vermißte Gut,
Noch den schon verlornen Mann zu lieben
Und zu saugen seines Herzens Blut.
   Ists um den geschehn,
   Muß nach andern gehn,
Und das junge Volk erliegt der Wut.

Schöner Jüngling, kannst nicht länger leben!
Du versiechest nun an diesem Ort.
Meine Kette hab ich dir gegeben;
Deine Locke nehm ich mit mir fort.
   Sieh sie an genau!
   Morgen bist du grau,
Und nur braun erscheinst du wieder dort.

Höre, Mutter, nun die letzte Bitte:
Einen Scheiterhaufen schichte du!
Öffne meine bange kleine Hütte,
Bring in Flammen Liebende zur Ruh!
   Wenn der Funke sprüht,
   Wenn die Asche glüht,
Eilen wir den alten Göttern zu."

"He, this youth, was pledged to me by token,
When still Venus' temples graced the land.
But thy word, O mother, thou hast broken,
At a false, and foreign vow's command!
Yet no god forbears
When a mother swears,
To refuse her daughter's promised hand.

"From the silent graveyard I am driven,
Still to seek the joys I missed, – though dust – ,
Still to love him, who from me was riven,
Suck his life-blood from his heart with gust.
Once he is destroyed,
Others are decoyed,
And the young fall victims to my lust.

"Handsome youth, to death thou hast awoken!
Thou wilt pine away here, in despond.
I have given thee my chain as token,
And I take thy lock of hair as bond.
Look at it today,
Morrow finds thee gray,
Brown-haired thou appear'st in the beyond.

"Mother, this my last wish, is compelling:
Build a pyre! Let this be thy aim!
Open up my small and narrow dwelling,
Lay the lovers to their rest in flame!
While the sparks still fly,
Ere the embers die,
We, above, the ancient gods acclaim."

Helen Kurz Roberts

DER GOTT UND DIE BAJADERE

Mahadöh, der Herr der Erde,
Kommt herab zum sechstenmal,
Daß er unsersgleichen werde,
Mitzufühlen Freud und Qual.
Er bequemt sich, hier zu wohnen,
Läßt sich alles selbst geschehn.
Soll er strafen oder schonen,
Muß er Menschen menschlich sehn.
Und hat er die Stadt sich als Wandrer betrachtet,
Die Großen belauert, auf Kleine geachtet,
Verläßt er sie abends, um weiterzugehn.

Als er nun hinausgegangen,
Wo die letzten Häuser sind,
Sieht er, mit gemalten Wangen,
Ein verlornes schönes Kind.
„Grüß dich, Jungfrau!" – „Dank der Ehre!
Wart, ich komme gleich hinaus." –
„Und wer bist du?" – „Bajadere,
Und dies ist der Liebe Haus."
Sie rührt sich, die Zimbeln zum Tanze zu schlagen;
Sie weiß sich so lieblich im Kreise zu tragen,
Sie neigt sich und biegt sich und reicht ihm den Strauß.

Schmeichelnd zieht sie ihn zur Schwelle,
Lebhaft ihn ins Haus hinein.
„Schöner Fremdling, lampenhelle
Soll sogleich die Hütte sein.
Bist du müd, ich will dich laben,
Lindern deiner Füße Schmerz.
Was du willst, das sollst du haben,
Ruhe, Freuden oder Scherz."
Sie lindert geschäftig geheuchelte Leiden.
Der Göttliche lächelt; er siehet mit Freuden
Durch tiefes Verderben ein menschliches Herz.

THE GOD AND THE BAYADEER

Mahadeva, great god Siva,
Has returned to earth again,
To be mortal with us mortals,
Know, as we know, joy and pain.
He agrees to dwell amongst us,
Take his lot whatever it be:
For, to punish men or spare them,
He must see men humanly.
And after the pilgrim has roamed through the city,
Has spied on the great, watched the wretched with pity,
He leaves before dark. There is much yet to see.

Reaching now the distant outskirts,
Where the rows of homes grow thin,
He perceives in gaudy raiment
A forsaken child of sin.
"Greetings, maiden." – "Sir, I thank you,
And I bid you stay and rest." –
"But who are you?" – "Bayadeer, Sir,
In this house you are love's guest."
And marking the rhythm with cymbalets ringing,
She gracefully dances through circling and swinging
And hands him the flowers she wore on her breast.

And she urges with caresses,
Bids him enter, goads him on.
"Handsome stranger, lamplit friendly
Will my cottage be anon.
You are weary. I will soothe you.
Will refresh and comfort you . . .
Ask for rest, diversion, pleasure,
All your bidding will I do."
She zealously nurses the ills he is feigning.
He cannot help smiling. With joy he sees reigning
In bawdy surroundings a heart warm and true.

Und er fordert Sklavendienste;
Immer heitrer wird sie nur,
Und des Mädchens frühe Künste
Werden nach und nach Natur.
Und so stellet auf die Blüte
Bald und bald die Frucht sich ein:
Ist Gehorsam im Gemüte,
Wird nicht fern die Liebe sein.
Aber, sie schärfer und schärfer zu prüfen,
Wählet der Kenner der Höhen und Tiefen
Lust und Entsetzen und grimmige Pein.

Und er küßt die bunten Wangen,
Und sie fühlt der Liebe Qual,
Und das Mädchen steht gefangen,
Und sie weint zum erstenmal;
Sinkt zu seinen Füßen nieder,
Nicht um Wollust noch Gewinst,
Ach, und die gelenken Glieder,
Sie versagen allen Dienst!
Und so zu des Lagers vergnüglicher Feier
Bereiten den dunklen behaglichen Schleier
Die nächtlichen Stunden, das schöne Gespinst.

Spät entschlummert unter Scherzen,
Früh erwacht nach kurzer Rast,
Findet sie an ihrem Herzen
Tot den vielgeliebten Gast.
Schreiend stürzt sie auf ihn nieder;
Aber nicht erweckt sie ihn,
Und man trägt die starren Glieder
Bald zur Flammengrube hin.
Sie höret die Priester, die Totengesänge,
Sie raset und rennet und teilet die Menge.
„Wer bist du? was drängt zu der Grube dich hin?"

He exacts a slave's performance.
She reacts with fairer cheer:
What were skills once of her calling
Now as nature's gifts appear.
And thus follows upon blossom
By and by the ripened fruit.
Where obedience marks the spirit,
Love is ready to take root.
But wishing to test her by keener devices,
He chooses, from knowledge of virtues and vices,
Delight first, then terror, and anguish to boot.

He enraptures her with kisses,
And she tastes love's bitter core.
And she stands enthralled and weeping:
Never did she weep before.
On her knees she falls before him,
Not for profit nor for lust.
Oh, her limbs lost all their sinew
Cringing helpless in the dust.
And thus, to envelop the rites of their pleasure,
Are woven the veils of the night's warming leisure
By hours of darkness, rewarding their trust.

Sleep comes late when lovers banter.
Yet, she needs but little rest. –
In her arms lies, as she wakens,
Dead the much-beloved guest.
And she throws herself upon him,
But no screams can halt his flight.
And they take the lifeless body
To the flame pit's somber site.
Her ear hears the priests intoning their dirges.
And forth through the crowd in frenzy she surges. –
"Who is she?—What gives her, to be here, a right?"

Bei der Bahre stürzt sie nieder,
Ihr Geschrei durchdringt die Luft:
,,Meinen Gatten will ich wieder!
Und ich such' ihn in der Gruft.
Soll zu Asche mir zerfallen
Dieser Glieder Götterpracht?
Mein! er war es, mein vor allen!
Ach, nur eine süße Nacht!"
Es singen die Priester: Wir tragen die Alten
Nach langem Ermatten und spätem Erkalten,
Wir tragen die Jugend, noch eh sie's gedacht.

,,Höre deiner Priester Lehre:
Dieser war dein Gatte nicht.
Lebst du doch als Bajadere,
Und so hast du keine Pflicht.
Nur dem Körper folgt der Schatten
In das stille Totenreich;
Nur die Gattin folgt dem Gatten:
Das ist Pflicht und Ruhm zugleich.
Ertöne, Drommete, zu heiliger Klage!
O nehmet, ihr Götter, die Zierde der Tage,
O nehmet den Jüngling in Flammen zu euch!"

So das Chor, das ohn Erbarmen
Mehret ihres Herzens Not;
Und mit ausgestreckten Armen
Springt sie in den heißen Tod.
Doch der Götterjüngling hebet
Aus der Flamme sich empor,
Und in seinen Armen schwebet
Die Geliebte mit hervor.
Es freut sich die Gottheit der reuigen Sünder;
Unsterbliche heben verlorene Kinder
Mit feurigen Armen zum Himmel empor.

By the bier she falls exhausted.
Yet her voice rings through the air:
"Give me, give me back my husband:
Death, release him from your lair. –
Shall the flames reduce to ashes
This proud body's godly sight? –
Mine he was – and no one other's –
Oh, but for one blessed night."
The priests proceed chanting: "The aged we carry
Whose flickering flame has no force left to tarry.
We carry the young, though their star shone still bright.

"Hear now, what your priests will teach you:
Husband he was not to you,
For you lead a bayadeer's life,
Owe to no one to be true.
Only shadow follows body
When it goes from where it came.
Only wife may follow husband.
That is duty; that is fame.
Let sound now the trumpet in awesome lamenting.
O gods, by your verdict which knows no relenting,
Take back your ephemeral gift in this flame."

Thus the chorus without pity
Multiplies her heart's despair.
And with outstretched arms she plunges
To her death in guttering glare.
But the beauteous god-youth rises
From the flames to realms above.
In his arms he carries with him
Bayadeer who bore him love.
The gods look with favor on penitent sinners.
They carry the wayward as ultimate winners
In fiery embraces to heavens above.

Alexander Gode

LYNKEUS DER TÜRMER

Zum Sehen geboren,
Zum Schauen bestellt,
Dem Turme geschworen,
Gefällt mir die Welt.
Ich blick in die Ferne,
Ich seh in der Näh
Den Mond und die Sterne,
Den Wald und das Reh.
So seh ich in allen
Die ewige Zier,
Und wie mirs gefallen,
Gefall ich auch mir.
Ihr glücklichen Augen,
Was je ihr gesehn,
Es sei, wie es wolle,
Es war doch so schön!

LYNCEUS THE WARDEN

Conceived to be seeing,
Appointed to sight,
The tower my being,
The world my delight.
I peer in the distance,
I see what is near,
The heavens' persistence,
The fleet-footed deer.
And as I find measure
In all that I view,
I view it with pleasure
And so myself too.
Ye eyes I call blessed,
Of all things ye see
The lasting remembrance
Their beauty will be.

Alexander Gode

SYMBOLUM

Die Zukunft decket
Schmerzen und Glücke
Schrittweis dem Blicke,
Doch ungeschrecket
Dringen wir vorwärts.

Und schwer und ferne
Hängt eine Hülle
Mit Ehrfurcht. – Stille
Ruhn oben die Sterne
Und unten die Gräber.

Doch rufen von drüben
Die Stimmen der Geister,
Die Stimmen der Meister:
„Versäumt nicht zu üben
Die Kräfte des Guten!

Hier flechten sich Kronen
In ewiger Stille,
Die sollen mit Fülle
Die Tätigen lohnen!
Wir heißen euch hoffen!"

SYMBOLUM

The future holds hidden
Blessings and sorrows
In rows of tomorrows. –
Undaunted, unbidden
We keep pressing forward.

Heavy and far
Of awe a curtain.
Star beyond star
Above. And certain
The graves below.

But voices we hallow
Of masters preceding
Invoke our heeding:
"Let never lie fallow
The forces of good.

We gather forever
In infinite calm
The laurel, the palm
For lives of endeavor –
And bid you have hope."

Alexander Gode

SPRÜCHE

Geheimnisvoll am lichten Tag
Läßt sich Natur des Schleiers nicht berauben,
Und was sie deinem Geist nicht offenbaren mag,
Das zwingst du ihr nicht ab mit Hebeln und mit Schrauben.

Jesus fühlte rein und dachte
Nur den einen Gott im Stillen;
Wer ihn selbst zum Gotte machte,
Kränkte seinen heilgen Willen.

Laß nur die Sorge sein,
Das gibt sich alles schon;
Und fällt der Himmel ein,
Kommt doch eine Lerche davon.

Mann mit zugeknöpften Taschen,
Dir tut niemand was zulieb.
Hand wird nur von Hand gewaschen:
Wenn du nehmen willst, so gib!

Wenn ein kluger Mann der Frau befiehlt,
Dann sei es um ein Großes gespielt;
Will die Frau dem Mann befehlen,
So muß sie das Große im Kleinen wählen.

Welche Frau hat einen guten Mann
Der sieht man's am Gesicht wohl an.

Denn wir können die Kinder nach unserem Sinne nicht formen;
So wie Gott sie uns gab, so muß man sie haben und lieben,
Sie erziehen aufs beste und jeglichen lassen gewähren.

SAYINGS

Mysterious in light of day,
Her veils doth Nature freely loosen never,
And all the secrets she will not to thee display
Thou shalt not worm away from her with prize and lever.

Pure was Jesus in his passion,
In his heart but one God serving;
Who of him a God would fashion
From his sacred will is swerving.

Forsake your worries all –
You have come through many a scrape –
And should the heavens fall,
One lark is sure to escape.

Button not thy pockets, brother,
None will thee a kindness give;
One hand's washed but by another,
Thou must give, wouldst thou receive!

When a shrewd man his wife command,
Let major issues be at hand;
But would a wife command her spouse,
The big within the little she must choose.

By a wife's face it may be known
That a good husband she doth own.

Children can scarcely be fashioned to meet with our likes and our
   purpose.
Just as God did us give them, so must we hold them and love
   them,
Nurture and teach them to fullness and leave them to be what
   they are.

Wer Wissenschaft und Kunst besitzt,
Hat auch Religion.
Wer jene beiden nicht besitzt,
Der habe Religion.

Müsset im Naturbetrachten
Immer eins wie alles achten:
Nichts ist drinnen, nichts ist draußen:
Denn was innen, das ist außen.
So ergreifet ohne Säumnis
Heilig öffentlich Geheimnis.

Wär' nicht das Auge sonnenhaft,
Nie könnte es die Sonn' erblicken
Wär' nicht in uns des Gottes eig'ne Kraft,
Wie könnt' uns Göttliches entzücken?

Was hieße wohl die Natur ergründen? –
Gott ebenso außen wie innen zu finden.

Was wär' ein Gott, der nur von außen stieße,
Im Kreis das All am Finger laufen ließe?
Ihm ziemt's, die Welt im Innern zu bewegen,
Natur in Sich, Sich in Natur zu hegen,
So daß, was in Ihm lebt und webt und ist,
Nie Seine Kraft, nie Seinen Geist vermißt.

Im Atemholen sind zweierlei Gnaden:
Die Luft einziehen, sich ihrer entladen;
Jenes bedrängt, dieses erfrischt;
So wunderbar ist das Leben gemischt.
Du danke Gott, wenn er dich preßt,
Und dank ihm, wenn er dich wieder entläßt.

He has religion
Who has art and science.
Who has not art nor science,
Needs have religion.

Heinz Norden

In your nature observation
One and all want equal station.
Nothing's inside, nothing's outside,
For the inside is the outside.
Grasp without procrastination
Patent-occult revelation.

Were not the eye born of the sun,
The sun could not by it be sighted.
Had our life not in God's strength begun,
How could by things divine we be delighted?

What is it we probers of Nature are seeking? –
Out there the God whom within we hear speaking!

What would a god be who but gave the world
A push to have it spin around His finger?
Him it behooves to move things from within
Comprising Nature and comprised by Her,
So that what in Him grows and flows and is
Must share the strength and spirit that are His.

In taking breath thou hast two kinds of blessing:
The air intracting, the air egressing.
The one feels anxious, the other refreshed.
Thus strangely too is thy life enmeshed.
Thou thank thy God Which presses thee;
And thank him further when He sets thee free.

Freudvoll
Und leidvoll,
Gedankenvoll sein,
Langen
Und bangen
In schwebender Pein,
Himmelhoch jauchzend,
Zum Tode betrübt –
Glücklich allein
Ist die Seele, die liebt.

Das Alter ist ein höflich Mann:
Einmal übers andre klopft er an,
Aber nun sagt niemand: Herein!
Und vor der Türe will er nicht sein.
Da klinkt er auf, tritt ein so schnell,
Und nun heißts, er sei ein grober Gesell.

Nie verläßt uns der Irrtum, doch ziehet ein höher Bedürfnis
Immer den strebenden Geist leise zur Wahrheit hinan.

Wer mit dem Leben spielt,
Kommt nie zurecht;
Wer sich nicht selbst befiehlt,
Bleibt immer ein Knecht.

Vergebens werden ungebundne Geister
nach der Vollendung reiner Höhe streben.
Wer Großes will, muß sich zusammenraffen.
In der Beschränkung zeigt sich erst der Meister,
und das Gesetz nur kann uns Freiheit geben.

Willst du ins Unendliche schreiten,
Geh im Endlichen nach allen Seiten.

Gladdened
And saddened
In thoughtful refrain,
Worried
And sorried
In lingering pain,
Cheered to high heaven,
Depressed to deep gloom,
Happy is fain
But a soul in love's bloom.

Age is a very courteous chap.
Knocks on the door with many a rap.
But bid him in no one does care.
And since he finds it cold out there,
At length he slips in quick and sure.
And now we call him a beastly boor.

Never will error release us, but always transcendent endeavor
Leads on the mind which persists, nearer – most gently – to truth.

Who lives by sleight of hand
Is bound to fall.
Who fails in self-command
Remains a thrall.

It is in vain when talent loath of bridle
Tries to attain the crown of full perfection.
He who aims high must gladly brook the harness:
To prove himself the master needs restriction,
And rule alone can give a man his freedom.

Wilt thou into infinities wander,
Roam through the finite hither and yonder.

Volk und Knecht und Überwinder,
Sie gestehn zu jeder Zeit:
Höchstes Glück der Erdenkinder
Sei nur die Persönlichkeit.
Jedes Leben sei zu führen,
Wenn man sich nicht selbst vermißt;
Alles könne man verlieren,
Wenn man bliebe, was man ist.

Ja! diesem Sinne bin ich ganz ergeben,
Das ist der Weisheit letzter Schluß:
Nur der verdient sich Freiheit wie das Leben,
Der täglich sie erobern muß.

Schaff, das Tagwerk meiner Hände,
Hohes Glück, daß ich's vollende!
Laß, o laß mich nicht ermatten!
Nein, es sind nicht leere Träume:
Jetzt nur Stangen, diese Bäume
Geben einst noch Frucht und Schatten.

Those in bondage, those in power,
All men of all times agree
That no fortune can be greater
Than man's personality,
That no life deserves man's scorning
If he, what he is, remains,
That no loss is worth his mourning
If his self he but retains.

This I believe with passionate obsession
And call it wisdom's ultimate advice:
None keeps of life and liberty possession,
But daily pays in sweat and toil their price.

Give me – bliss of daily striving –
Give me trust it will be thriving!
Keep my strength, keep it from fading!
No, it is not idle dreaming:
Spindly stalks these trees now seeming
Will in time give fruit and shading.

Alexander Gode

Friedrich Schiller

DAS GLÜCK

Selig, welchen die Götter, die gnädigen, vor der Geburt schon
  Liebten, welchen als Kind Venus im Arme gewiegt,
Welchem Phöbus die Augen, die Lippen Hermes gelöset
  Und das Siegel der Macht Zeus auf die Stirne gedrückt!
Ein erhabenes Los, ein göttliches, ist ihm gefallen,
  Schon vor des Kampfes Beginn sind ihm die Schläfen bekränzt.
Ihm ist, eh er es lebte, das volle Leben gerechnet,
  Eh er die Mühe bestand, hat er die Charis erlangt.

Groß zwar nenn' ich den Mann, der, sein eigner Bildner und Schöpfer,
  Durch der Tugend Gewalt selber die Parze bezwingt;
Aber nicht erzwingt er das Glück, und was ihm die Charis
  Neidisch geweigert, erringt nimmer der strebende Mut.
Vor Unwürdigem kann dich der Wille, der ernste, bewahren,
  Alles Höchste, es kommt frei von den Göttern herab.
Wie die Geliebte dich liebt, so kommen die himmlischen Gaben;
  Oben in Jupiters Reich herrscht, wie in Amors, die Gunst.
Neigungen haben die Götter, sie lieben der grünenden Jugend
  Lockigte Scheitel, es zieht Freude die Fröhlichen an.
Nicht der Sehende wird von ihrer Erscheinung beseligt,
  Ihrer Herrlichkeit Glanz hat nur der Blinde geschaut.
Gern erwählen sie sich der Einfalt kindliche Seele,
  In das bescheidne Gefäß schließen sie Göttliches ein.
Ungehofft sind sie da und täuschen die stolze Erwartung,
  Keines Bannes Gewalt zwinget die Freien herab.
Wem er geneigt, dem sendet der Vater der Menschen und Götter
  Seinen Adler herab, trägt ihn zu himmlischen Höhn.

THE GIFTS OF FORTUNE

Blessed whom, ere he was born, the gods for their favors had chosen,
   Whom, while he was but a child, Venus held up in her arms.
Phoebus opens his eyes, his lips are untied by Hermes,
   And the emblem of might Zeus imprints on his brow.
Truly, sublime is his prospect. The fate that befell him is godlike.
   His is the victor's crown long ere the fray has begun;
Long ere he starts on his journey, its goal is reckoned
      accomplished;
   Ere he has proven his worth, safe he stands sheltered in grace.

Great, to be sure, will I call the other who – self-made and
      self-trained –
   Alters, by virtue's strength, even the Moira's decree.
Never the gifts of Fortune will thus be compelled. What is given
   Only by grace must remain outside the pale of man's will.
Earnest endeavor can help one to vanquish the powers of evil,
   But the ultimate good unbidden descends from on high.
Heaven bestows its gifts as love is bestowed by lovers:
   Favor rules Cupid's realm, likewise the realm of Zeus.
Think not the gods impartial. The curls of youth may bewitch them.
   Gay in their hearts themselves, fain with the gay they consort.
Not the keen-eyed observer is granted the bliss to behold them;
   Only the unknowing blind witness their splendorous light.
Often they choose for their gifts the simple soul of the childlike,
   Casting in humblest forms substance of heavenly kin.
Coming where least awaited, they foil him who proudly expects them:
   There is no magic, no spell potent to cast them in bonds.
Whom the Father of men and Immortals has chosen his minion
   He bids his eagle seek out, carry to heavenly heights.

Unter die Menge greift er mit Eigenwillen, und welches
    Haupt ihm gefället, um das flicht er mit liebender Hand
Jetzt den Lorbeer und jetzt die herrschaftgebende Binde,
    Krönte doch selber den Gott nur das gewogene Glück.

Vor dem Glücklichen her tritt Phöbus, der pythische Sieger,
    Und, der die Herzen bezwingt, Amor, der lächelnde Gott.
Vor ihm ebnet Poseidon das Meer, sanft gleitet des Schiffes
    Kiel, das den Cäsar führt und sein allmächtiges Glück.
Ihm zu Füßen legt sich der Leu, das brausende Delphin
    Steigt aus den Tiefen, und fromm beut es den Rücken ihm an.

Zürne dem Glücklichen nicht, daß den leichten Sieg ihm die Götter
    Schenken, daß aus der Schlacht Venus den Liebling entrückt.
Ihn, den die Lächelnde rettet, den Göttergeliebten beneid' ich,

    Jenen nicht, dem sie mit Nacht deckt den verdunkelten Blick.
War er weniger herrlich, Achilles, weil ihm Hephästos
    Selbst geschmiedet den Schild und das verderbliche Schwert?
Weil um den sterblichen Mann der große Olymp sich beweget?
    Das verherrlichet ihn, daß ihn die Götter geliebt,
Daß sie sein Zürnen geehrt und, Ruhm dem Liebling zu geben,
    Hellas' bestes Geschlecht stürzten zum Orkus hinab.
Zürne der Schönheit nicht, daß sie schön ist, daß sie verdienstlos,
    Wie der Lilie Kelch prangt durch der Venus Geschenk!
Laß sie die Glückliche sein; du schaust sie, du bist der Beglückte!

    Wie sie ohne Verdienst glänzt, so entzücket sie dich.
Freue dich, daß die Gabe des Lieds vom Himmel herabkommt,
    Daß der Sänger dir singt, was ihn die Muse gelehrt:
Weil der Gott ihn beseelt, so wird er dem Hörer zum Gotte;
    Weil er der Glückliche ist, kannst du der Selige sein.
Auf dem geschäftigen Markt, da führe Themis die Waage,
    Und es messe der Lohn streng an der Mühe sich ab;

Guided by whim or fancy, the god finds the one among many
    Whom he decides to like, and with a loving hand
Crowns with laurels or fillet of power the head he has chosen,
    For, he himself wears his crown only by Fortune's grace.

Smoothed is the path of the fortunate mortal by Phoebus Apollo
    And the subduer of hearts, Amor, the smiling god.
Neptune quiets the ocean before him, and blithely his vessel –
    "Caesar aboard and his luck" – follows his charted course.
Gently the lion lies down at his feet, and the agile dolphin
    Pushes its back into view, ready to serve as his mount.

Do not resent that the gods grant the favored few effortless triumphs
    Or that whom Venus prefers safely she whisks from the fight.
Worthy of praise deems the world whom the smiling goddess has
       rescued,
    Paying the other no heed whom she let sink to the shades.
Do we account Achilles' glory impaired since Hephaestus
    Fashioned his mighty shield and his destructive sword,
Since for this one mortal human all of Olympus is stirring?
    No, it glorifies him that he is loved by the gods,
That they would honor his wrath, and, for the sake of his glory,
    Plunge the flower of Greece into the Hadean night.
Do not resent that beauty's beauty stems from no merit,
    That it is Venus's gift, free as the blossoms of Spring.
Let beauty enjoy its good fortune. Behold it and share the
       enjoyment.
    Undeserved are its charms. So is your power to see.
Let us rejoice that the gift of song has descended from heaven,
    That the poet, for us, sings what he learned from the Muse.
Holding his fief from a god, he appears as a god to us hearers,
    Being by Fortune endowed, bliss he reflects upon us.
In the affairs of the market let Themis hold sway with her balance.
    There the weight of the toil measures by rights the reward.

Aber die Freude ruft nur ein Gott auf sterbliche Wangen,
  Wo kein Wunder geschieht, ist kein Beglückter zu sehn.

Alles Menschliche muß erst werden und wachsen und reifen,
  Und von Gestalt zu Gestalt führt es die bildende Zeit;
Aber das Glückliche siehest du nicht, das Schöne nicht werden,
  Fertig von Ewigkeit her steht es vollendet vor dir.
Jede irdische Venus ersteht, wie die erste des Himmels,
  Eine dunkle Geburt, aus dem unendlichen Meer;
Wie die erste Minerva, so tritt, mit der Ägis gerüstet,
  Aus des Donnerers Haupt jeder Gedanke des Lichts.

Not so with joy. It appears when a god has decreed its appearance:
  Only a miracle can conjure its warmth to men's hearts.

Everything human must slowly arise, must unfold, and must ripen:
  Ever from phase to phase plastic time leads it on.
But neither beauty nor fortune are ever born into being:
  Perfect ere time began, perfect they face us today.
Every Venus on earth emerges, as did the divine one,
  As an occult event from the infinite sea.
Perfect, like the divine Minerva, equipped with the aegis,
  So every light-bearing thought springs from the Thunderer's head.

Alexander Gode

NÄNIE

Auch das Schöne muß sterben! Das Menschen und Götter bezwinget
  Nicht die eherne Brust rührt es des stygischen Zeus.
Einmal nur erweichte die Liebe den Schattenbeherrscher,
  Und an derSchwelle noch, streng, rief er zurück sein Geschenk.
Nicht stillt Aphrodite dem schönen Knaben die Wunde,
  Die in den zierlichen Leib grausam der Eber geritzt.
Nicht errettet den göttlichen Held die unsterbliche Mutter,
  Wann er, am skäischen Tor fallend, sein Schicksal erfüllt.
Aber sie steigt aus dem Meer mit allen Töchtern des Nereus,
  Und die Klage hebt an um den verherrlichten Sohn.
Siehe! Da weinen die Götter, es weinen die Göttinnen alle,
  Daß das Schöne vergeht, daß das Vollkommene stirbt.
Auch ein Klaglied zu sein im Mund der Geliebten, ist herrlich,
  Denn das Gemeine geht klanglos zum Orkus hinab.

NENIA

Also the beautiful dies. – Its spell binds all men and immortals
  Save one: the Stygian Zeus. Armored in steel is his breast.
Once, only did soften a lover the ruler of Hades.
  Yet, ere the threshold was reached, sternly he canceled his gift.
As Aphrodite stills not the gaping wounds of Adonis
  Which on the beautiful youth, hunted, the wild boar inflicts,
So the immortal Thetis saves not her divine son Achilles
  When at the Scaean Gate, falling, he meets with his fate.
But from the sea she arises with all the daughters of Nereus,
  And they intone their lament for her transfigured son.
Lo, all the gods now are weeping and weeping is every goddess
  That the beautiful wanes, that the perfect must die.
Glory is also to be a song of sorrow of loved ones,
  For, what is vulgar goes down songless to echoless depths.

Alexander Gode

Friedrich Hölderlin

DA ICH EIN KNABE WAR

Da ich ein Knabe war,
Rettet' ein Gott mich oft
Vom Geschrei und der Rute der Menschen,
Da spielt' ich sicher und gut
Mit den Blumen des Hains,
Und die Lüftchen des Himmels
Spielten mit mir.

Und wie du das Herz
Der Pflanzen erfreust,
Wenn sie entgegen dir
Die zarten Arme strecken,

So hast du mein Herz erfreut,
Vater Helios! und, wie Endymion,
War ich dein Liebling,
Heilige Luna!

O all ihr treuen,
Freundlichen Götter!
Daß ihr wüßtet,
Wie euch meine Seele geliebt!

Zwar damals rief ich noch nicht
Euch mit Namen, auch ihr
Nanntet mich nie, wie die Menschen sich nennen,
Als kennten sie sich.

WHILE I WAS YET A BOY

While I was yet a boy
Some god often preserved me
From the clamor and rods of men;
Then safely and well I prayed
With the woodland flowers,
And the breezes of Heaven
Gamboled with me.

And as you delight
The heart of plants
That stretch their tender
Arms to meet you,

So you've rejoiced my heart,
Father Helios! And like Endymion
I was your little lover,
Holy Luna!

O all you faithful
Friendly Gods!
If you knew how
My soul loved you!

I did not then as yet
Call you by name, and also you
Never named me, as men, seeming to know,
Will name one another.

Doch kannt' ich euch besser,
Als ich je die Menschen gekannt,
Ich verstand die Stille des Äthers,
Der Menschen Worte verstand ich nie.

Mich erzog der Wohllaut
Des säuselnden Hains
Und lieben lernt' ich
Unter den Blumen.
Im Arme der Götter wuchs ich groß.

But you I knew better
Than ever I did mankind;
1 understood the Aether's quietness,
Never, though, the words of men.

I was nurtured by the harmony
Of rustling boughs
And learned among flowers
How to love.
In arms divine I grew to manhood.

Philip Allan Friedman

MENSCHENBEIFALL

Ist nicht heilig mein Herz, schöneren Lebens voll,
Seit ich liebe? warum achtetet ihr mich mehr,
Da ich stolzer und wilder,
Wortereicher und leerer war?

Ach! der Menge gefällt, was auf den Marktplatz taugt,
Und es ehret der Knecht nur den Gewaltsamen;
An das Göttliche glauben
Die allein, die es selber sind.

THE CROWD'S ACCLAIM

Is not my heart hallowed and filled with truer life
Since love came? Then why did ye value me more
When I was prouder and fiercer
Fuller of words, and emptier?

Yes – the crowds prefer what shines in the marketplace,
The menial eagerly crawls before the blusterer;
In the godly believe
Only those who are so themselves.

Martin Zwart

SOKRATES UND ALKIBIADES

„Warum huldigest du, heiliger Sokrates,
Diesem Jünglinge stets? Kennest du Größers nicht?
Warum siehet mit Liebe,
Wie auf Götter, dein Aug auf ihn?"   *

Wer das Tiefste gedacht, liebt das Lebendigste.
Hohe Tugend versteht, wer in die Welt geblickt,
Und es neigen die Weisen
Oft am Ende zu Schönem sich.

SOCRATES AND ALCIBIADES

Saintly Socrates, why do you favor
This youth incessantly? Know you nothing greater?
Why does your eye fasten
On him as on the gods with love?

Who most deeply has thought loves what is most alive;
High virtue he understands who on the world has gazed;
And often the sages
In the end bow to loveliness.

Palmer Hilty

ABENDPHANTASIE

Vor seiner Hütte ruhig im Schatten sitzt
Der Pflüger, dem Genügsamen raucht sein Herd.
Gastfreundlich tönt dem Wanderer im
Friedlichen Dorfe die Abendglocke.

Wohl kehren jetzt die Schiffer zum Hafen auch,
In fernen Städten fröhlich verrauscht des Markts
Geschäft'ger Lärm; in stiller Laube
Glänzt das gesellige Mahl den Freunden.

Wohin denn ich? Es leben die Sterblichen
Von Lohn und Arbeit; wechselnd in Müh' and Ruh'
Ist alles freudig; warum schläft denn
Nimmer nur mir in der Brust der Stachel?

Am Abendhimmel blühet ein Frühling auf;
Unzählig blühen die Rosen, und ruhig scheint
Die goldne Welt; o dorthin nehmt mich,
Purpurne Wolken! und möge droben

In Licht und Luft zerrinnen mir Lieb und Leid! —
Doch, wie verscheucht von törichter Bitte, flieht
Der Zauber; dunkel wird's, und einsam
Unter dem Himmel, wie immer, bin ich. —

Komm du nun, sanfter Schlummer! zu viel begehrt
Das Herz; doch endlich, Jugend, verglühst du ja,
Du ruhelose, träumerische!
Friedlich und heiter ist dann das Alter.

EVENING FANCY

The plowman sits in front of his shaded cot,
While evening smoke goes up from his frugal hearth.
The bell's note from the peaceful village
Rings friendly welcome to the traveller.

The boatmen doubtless now are returning too
To harbor, while in distant cities the busy hum
Of markets dies away; a friendly
Meal is laid out under quiet leafage.

But where shall I go? Men live alone by work
And wages, find their happiness turn by turn
In toil and rest; then why in my heart
Is there no sleep for the goad that pricks me?

A springtime blossoms now in the evening sky;
Unnumbered roses blossom, the golden world
Seems all at rest; oh, purple cloud banks,
Take me up there, and in light and ether

Let love and pain dissolve, and be swept away!
But now as though dispelled by my foolish prayer
The magic flees; night falls, and lonely
Under the heavens I stand, as always.

Then *you* come, gentle sleep! For my heart desires
Too much. But youth, your fire must at last burn out,
You never-resting, ardent dreamer!
Peaceful and cheerful old age comes after.

W. Edward Brown

GEH UNTER, SCHÖNE SONNE

Geh unter, schöne Sonne, sie achteten
Nur wenig dein, sie kannten dich, Heilige, nicht,
Denn mühelos und stille bist du
Über den Mühsamen aufgegangen.

Mir gehst du freundlich unter und auf, o Licht!
Und wohl erkennt mein Auge dich, herrliches!
Denn göttlich stille ehren lernt' ich,
Da Diotima den Sinn mir heilte.

O du, des Himmels Botin! wie lauscht' ich dir!
Dir, Diotima! Liebe! wie sah von dir
Zum goldnen Tage dieses Auge
Glänzend und dankend empor. Da rauschten

Lebendiger die Quellen, es atmeten
Der dunkeln Erde Blüten mich liebend an,
Und lächelnd über Silberwolken
Neigte sich segnend herab der Äther.

DESCEND, BEAUTIFUL SUN

Descend, beautiful sun; they have paid you
But small regard, holy one, have known you not,
Because your rising was effortless and quiet
Over laborious human beings.

For me you rise and set like a friend, O light!
My eyes indeed perceive your gloriousness!
For I've learned to worship divine calm
Since Diotima has healed my senses.

O you heavenly messenger! Love! Diotima!
How they turn from you, how I hearken
To greet the golden day above me,
These eyes shining and grateful! More lively

Sing the gurgling brooks, and the blossoming
Of dusky earth lovingly breathes on me
As smiling over silver cloudlets,
Down with a blessing bends the aether.

Philip Allan Friedman

HYPERIONS SCHICKSALSLIED

Ihr wandelt droben im Licht
Auf weichem Boden, selige Genien!
Glänzende Götterlüfte
Rühren euch leicht,
Wie die Finger der Künstlerin
Heilige Saiten.

Schicksallos, wie der schlafende
Säugling, atmen die Himmlischen;
Keusch bewahrt
In bescheidener Knospe,
Blühet ewig
Ihnen der Geist,
Und die seligen Augen
Blicken in stiller
Ewiger Klarheit.

Doch uns ist gegeben,
Auf keiner Stätte zu ruhn,
Es schwinden, es fallen
Die leidenden Menschen
Blindlings von einer
Stunde zur andern,
Wie Wasser von Klippe
Zu Klippe geworfen,
Jahrlang ins Ungewisse hinab.

HYPERION'S SONG OF FATE

You roam above in the light
On yielding meadows, blessed genii!
Brilliant ethereal breezes
Gently caress you
As by virginal fingering
Of sanctified strings.

Fatelessly, like the slumbering
Suckling breathe the celestials;
Chastely sheathed
In most modest petals
Blooms their never-
Withering spirit,
And their blissful eyes
Gaze with serene
Eternal clarity.

To us, though, is granted
No place to find for repose;
The suffering human beings
Fall and vanish,
Blind things from one hour
On to another,
As waters are hurled
From boulder to boulder
Down through the years to nowhere known.

Philip Allan Friedman

AN DIE PARZEN

Nur einen Sommer gönnt, ihr Gewaltigen!
Und einen Herbst zu reifem Gesange mir,
　　Daß williger mein Herz, vom süßen
　　　　Spiele gesättigt, dann mir sterbe!

Die Seele, der im Leben ihr göttlich Recht
Nicht ward, sie ruht auch drunten im Orkus nicht;
　　Doch ist mir einst das Heilge, das am
　　　　Herzen mir liegt, das Gedicht, gelungen:

Willkommen dann, o Stille der Schattenwelt!
Zufrieden bin ich, wenn auch mein Saitenspiel
　　Mich nicht hinabgeleitet: einmal
　　　　Lebt ich wie Götter, und mehr bedarfs nicht.

TO THE PARCAE

A single summer grant me, ye Mighty Ones!,
And time wherein to harvest the ripened song,
That willingly my heart, thus slaked in
Rhythmical sweetness may heed the Summons.

The soul whose godlike due is denied it in
This life, finds no repose in the realm of shades.
Yet once the sacred trust I have at
Heart is accomplished – the poem spoken –

Be welcome then, O quiet land of death.
At peace I rest, albeit my lyre cannot
Go with me down to Orcus. Once I
Lived like the gods, and nought else is needed.

Alexander Gode

HÄLFTE DES LEBENS

Mit gelben Birnen hänget
Und voll mit wilden Rosen
Das Land in den See,
Ihr holden Schwäne,
Und trunken von Küssen
Tunkt ihr das Haupt
Ins heilignüchterne Wasser.

Weh mir, wo nehm ich, wenn
Es Winter ist, die Blumen, und wo
Den Sonnenschein
Und Schatten der Erde?
Die Mauern stehn
Sprachlos und kalt, im Winde
Klirren die Fahnen.

HALF OF LIFE

Filled with yellow pears
And with wild roses,
The landscape hangs in the lake,
O gentle swans;
And drunk with kisses
You dip your heads
In the sacred sober water.

Alas, whence shall I take,
When it is winter, flowers and
Whence sunshine
And shadows on the ground?
The walls stand
Dumb and cold, the weathercocks
Whirr in the wind.

Willard R. Trask
Alexander Gode

LEBENSALTER

Ihr Städte des Euphrats!
Ihr Gassen von Palmyra!
Ihr Säulenwälder in der Ebne der Wüste,
Was seid ihr?
Euch hat die Kronen,
Dieweil ihr über die Grenze
Der Odmenden seid gegangen,
Von Himmlischen der Rauchdampf und
Hinweg das Feuer genommen;
Jetzt aber sitz' ich unter Wolken (deren
Ein jedes ein Ruh' hat eigen), unter
Wohleingerichteten Eichen, auf
Der Heide des Rehs, und fremd
Erscheinen und gestorben mir
Der Seligen Geister.

AGE

Ye cities on the Euphrates!
Ye streets of Palmyra!
Ye forests of pillars in the level desert! –
What are ye?
Your crowns –
Ye having gone beyond
The limits of what has breath –
The smokes and mists of heaven
And fire have taken away.
But I now sit under clouds (of which
Each has its own peace), under
Well-ordered oaks, on
The roebuck's heath; and alien
They come before me, and long dead,
The spirits of the blessed.

Willard R. Trask

Das Angenehme dieser Welt hab ich genossen
Der Jugend Freuden sind wie lang, wie lang! verflossen.
April und Mai und Junius sind ferne,
Ich bin nichts mehr, ich lebe nicht mehr gerne.

The pleasantness of life was mine once undiminished
The joys of youth have passed, passed long ago, they're finished.
April and May and June, how fast they're fleeing,
I'm nothing now and tired of my being.

Meno Spann

DER HERBST

Dies ist der Herbst: der – bricht dir noch das Herz!
Fliege fort! fliege fort! –
Die Sonne schleicht zum Berg
und steigt und steigt
und ruht bei jedem Schritt.

Was ward die Welt so welk!
Auf müd gespannten Fäden spielt
der Wind sein Lied.
Die Hoffnung floh –
er klagt ihr nach.

Dies ist der Herbst: der – bricht dir noch das Herz!
Fliege fort! fliege fort!
O Frucht des Baums,
du zitterst, fällst?
Welch ein Geheimnis lehrte dich die Nacht,
daß eisger Schauder deine Wange,
die Purpurwange deckt? –

Du schweigst, antwortest nicht?
Wer redet noch? – –
Dies ist der Herbst: der – bricht dir noch das Herz!
Fliege fort! fliege fort!
„Ich bin nicht schön"
– so spricht die Sternenblume –
„doch Menschen lieb ich
und Menschen tröst ich –
sie sollen jetzt noch Blumen sehn,
nach mir sich bücken,
ach! und mich brechen –
in ihrem Auge glänzet dann

FALL

This is the Fall, which yet will break your heart!
Fly away, fly away! –
The sun creeps to the hills
And climbs and climbs
And rests with every step.

How wilted grew the world!
On wearily strung threads the wind
Intunes its song.
Hope has fled,
Wind mourns for her.

This is the Fall, which yet will break your heart!
Fly away, fly away! –
Fruit of the tree,
You tremble, fall?
What secret must have taught to you the night
That icy shudders cover
Your cheek, the purple cheek?

You stay mute, you answer not?
Who is it speaks?
This is the Fall, which yet will break your heart!
Fly away, fly away! –
"I am not handsome,"
The aster tells me,
"Yet I love mankind
And comfort mankind,
They shall see flowers still now
And bend down for me
Alas! and pick me –
Then from their eyes remembrance

Erinnerung auf,
Erinnerung an Schöneres als ich: –
ich sehs, ich sehs – und sterbe so!" –

Dies ist der Herbst: der – bricht dir noch das Herz!
Fliege fort! fliege fort!

Glitters forth,
Remembrance of more handsome things than I: –
I see it, see it, and thus I die."

This is the Fall, which yet will break your heart!
Fly away, fly away!

Hedwig Hellmann

DER TOD

Er erschreckt uns,
Unser Retter der Tod. Sanft kommt er
Leis im Gewölke des Schlafs.

Aber er bleibt fürchterlich, und wir sehn nur
Nieder ins Grab, ob er gleich uns zur Vollendung
Führt aus Hüllen der Nacht hinüber
In der Erkenntnisse Land.

DEATH

He frightens us,
Our Deliverer Death. Softly he comes
Faint in the clouds of sleep.

But he remains frightful, and we look only
Down into the grave, though he lead us to the summit
Out of the veil of night, over
To the land of perception.

Lyn Goetze Snyder

Novalis

ICH SEHE DICH IN TAUSEND BILDERN

Ich sehe dich in tausend Bildern,
Maria, lieblich ausgedrückt,
Doch keins von allen kann dich schildern,
Wie meine Seele dich erblickt.

Ich weiß nur, daß der Welt Getümmel
Seitdem mir wie ein Traum verweht,
Und ein unnennbar süßer Himmel
Mir ewig im Gemüte steht.

OH BLESSED MARY

O blessed Mary, I have seen thy face
A thousand times portrayed most pleasingly,
And yet in all of these I cannot trace
The fulness that my soul once found in thee.

I only know that all the world's unrest
Has since, like dreams, been blown away,
And heavenly bliss that cannot be expressed
Forever in my heart has come to stay.

D. G. Wright

Unbekannter Dichter

Ich hab die Nacht geträumet
Wohl einen schweren Traum;
Es wuchs in meinem Garten
Ein Rosmarienbaum.

Der Kirchhof war der Garten,
Das Blumenbeet ein Grab,
Und von dem grünen Baume
Fiel Kron und Blüten ab.

Die Blüten tät ich sammeln
In einen goldnen Krug;
Der fiel mir aus den Händen,
Daß er in Stücke schlug.

Draus sah ich Perlen rinnen
Und Tröpflein rosenrot.
Was mag der Traum bedeuten?
Herzliebster, bist du tot?

Last night while I was dreaming
A nightmare haunted me;
I dreamed that in my garden
There grew a rosemary tree.

The garden was a graveyard,
A flowerbed the tomb,
And from the green tree falling
Came leaves, and flowers in bloom.

I gathered up the blossoms
Into a jug of gold.
It fell out of my fingers
And shattered a hundredfold.

I saw pearls running from it,
And droplets rosy red.
Ah, what can be the meaning?
My sweetest, are you dead?

D. G. Wright

Clemens Brentano

WIEGENLIED

Singet leise, leise, leise,
Singt ein flüsternd Wiegenlied,
Von dem Monde lernt die Weise,
Der so still am Himmel zieht.

Singt ein Lied so süß gelinde,
Wie die Quellen auf den Kieseln,
Wie die Bienen um die Linde
Summen, murmeln, flüstern, rieseln.

SLUMBER SONG

Softly, softly, sing a tune;
Sing a whispered lullaby;
Learn thy lay from Lady Moon,
Moving soundless through the sky.

Sing a song as sweetly sighing
As the springs on pebbles curling,
As the bees round linden flying
Humming, trickling, rustling, purling.

Anne Jennings

ABENDSTÄNDCHEN

Hör, es klagt die Flöte wieder
Und die kühlen Brunnen rauschen,
Golden wehn die Töne nieder –
Stille, stille, lass uns lauschen!

Holdes Bitten, mild Verlangen,
Wie es süß zum Herzen spricht!
Durch die Nacht, die mich umfangen,
Blickt zu mir der Töne Licht.

SERENADE

Hark, once more the flute's complaining,
And the rustling fountains glisten;
Golden strains are wafted downward –
Quiet, quiet! let us listen!

Gracious pleading, gentle longing,
To my heart they make their plea,
Through the dense night that surrounds me,
Light of music shines on me.

Anne Jennings

DER SPINNERIN LIED

Es sang vor langen Jahren
Wohl auch die Nachtigall,
Das war wohl süßer Schall,
Da wir zusammen waren.

Ich sing und kann nicht weinen
Und spinne so allein
Den Faden klar und rein,
Solang der Mond wird scheinen.

Da wir zusammen waren,
Da sang die Nachtigall,
Nun mahnet mich ihr Schall,
Daß du von mir gefahren.

So oft der Mond mag scheinen,
Gedenk ich dein allein,
Mein Herz ist klar und rein,
Gott wolle uns vereinen!

Seit du von mir gefahren,
Singt stets die Nachtigall,
Ich denk bei ihrem Schall,
Wie wir zusammen waren.

Gott wolle uns vereinen,
Hier spinn ich so allein,
Der Mond scheint klar und rein,
Ich sing und möchte weinen!

THE SPINSTRESS' SONG

Of yore, as now, aringing
Sweet sang the nightingale.
We heard the echo trail,
Each to the other clinging.

I sing to keep from weeping
And spin, all lonesome here,
The thread so pure and clear
Until the moon sets, sleeping.

Each to the other clinging
We heard the nightingale.
But now the echoes trail,
For you did leave me, singing.

Ere yet the moon sets sleeping,
My thoughts roam far from here.
My heart is pure and clear.
God join us in His keeping.

Since you did leave me, singing,
I hear the nightingale.
We heard the echoes trail,
Faintly together clinging.

God join us in His keeping.
I spin, all lonesome here,
The moon shines pure and clear,
I sing and would be weeping.

Alexander Gode

Justinus Kerner

POESIE

Poesie ist tiefes Schmerzen,
Und es kommt das echte Lied
Einzig aus dem Menschenherzen,
Das ein tiefes Leid durchglüht.

Doch die höchsten Poesien
Schweigen wie der höchste Schmerz,
Nur wie Geisterschatten ziehen
Stumm sie durchs gebrochne Herz.

POETRY

Poetry is deepest aching,
And the truest, purest strain
Only comes from man's heart breaking
In the glow of deepest pain.

But the silence of his grieving
Is the poet's highest art,
Soundlessly like shadows weaving
Through the ruins of his heart.

Martin Zwart

Ludwig Uhland

DES KNABEN BERGLIED

Ich bin vom Berg der Hirtenknab',•
Seh' auf die Schlösser all herab;
Die Sonne strahlt am ersten hier,
Am längsten weilet sie bei mir;
Ich bin der Knab' vom Berge!

Hier ist des Stromes Mutterhaus,
Ich trink' ihn frisch vom Stein heraus;
Er braust vom Fels in wildem Lauf,
Ich fang' ihn mit den Armen auf;
Ich bin der Knab' vom Berge!

Der Berg, der ist mein Eigentum,
Da ziehn die Stürme rings herum;
Und heulen sie von Nord und Süd,
So überschallt sie doch mein Lied:
Ich bin der Knab' vom Berge!

Sind Blitz und Donner unter mir,
So steh' ich hoch im Blauen hier;
Ich kenne sie und rufe zu:
„Laßt meines Vaters Haus in Ruh'!"
Ich bin der Knab' vom Berge!

Und wann die Sturmglock' einst erschallt,
Manch Feuer auf den Bergen wallt,
Dann steig' ich nieder, tret' ins Glied
Und schwing' mein Schwert und sing' mein Lied:
Ich bin der Knab' vom Berge!

THE LAD OF THE MOUNTAIN

I stand up here where storm winds blow,
Look on the castles down below;
I see the rising sun's first gleams,
I see its latest dying beams;
I am the lad of the mountain.

The stream's maternal home is here,
I drink its freshness crystal clear;
In wild career it bursts its bands,
I catch it when I fill my hands;
I am the lad of the mountain.

The mountain is my very own,
The storm clouds round about are blown;
Though winds from north and south may roar,
My song's but louder than before;
I am the lad of the mountain.

When lightning I can see below,
And thunder hear, 'tis then I know
I'm in the clear, blue sky and cry:
"Leave us in peace as you pass by"!
I am the lad of the mountain!

But when alarm bells warning ring,
When fires from the hilltops spring,
Then I'll go down my friends among,
And swing my sword and sing my song:
I am the lad of the mountain!

Francis Owen

FRÜHLINGSGLAUBE

Die linden Lüfte sind erwacht,
Sie säuseln und weben Tag und Nacht,
Sie schaffen an allen Enden.
O frischer Duft, o neuer Klang!
Nun, armes Herze, sei nicht bang!
Nun muß sich alles, alles wenden.

Die Welt wird schöner mit jedem Tag,
Man weiß nicht, was noch werden mag,
Das Blühen will nicht enden.
Es blüht das fernste, tiefste Tal:
Nun, armes Herz, vergiß der Qual!
Nun muß sich alles, alles wenden!

HOPE IN SPRINGTIME

The balmy breezes are aloft,
By day and night are wafting soft,
From near to far they range.
What fragrance, what new sound are here!
Hush, my poor heart, be without fear!
For now it all, it all must change.

The world grows fairer every day,
What's yet to come one cannot say,
It blooms in endless range:
Blooms deck the farthest dell and plain.
Hush, my poor heart, forget thy pain!
For now it all, it all must change.

Martin Zwart

AUF DEN TOD EINES KINDES

Du kamst, du gingst mit leiser Spur,
Ein flücht'ger Gast im Erdenland;
Woher? Wohin? Wir wissen nur:
Aus Gottes Hand in Gottes Hand.

"ON THE DEATH OF A CHILD"

You came, you went, a fleeting guest
Upon the earth you lightly trod.
From where to where? We only know:
From God into the hands of God.

Oliver Brown

Joseph von Eichendorff

DER FROHE WANDERSMANN

Wem Gott will rechte Gunst erweisen,
Den schickt er in die weite Welt;
Dem will er seine Wunder weisen
In Berg und Wald und Strom und Feld.

Die Trägen, die zu Hause liegen,
Erquicket nicht das Morgenrot;
Sie wissen nur von Kinderwiegen,
Von Sorgen, Last und Not um Brot.

Die Bächlein von den Bergen springen,
Die Lerchen schwirren hoch vor Lust,
Was sollt ich nicht mit ihnen singen
Aus voller Kehl und frischer Brust?

Den lieben Gott laß ich nur walten;
Der Bächlein, Lerchen, Wald und Feld
Und Erd und Himmel will erhalten,
Hat auch mein Sach aufs best bestellt!

THE JOYFUL TRAVELLER

The man whom God will show true favor,
He ushers forth to live his dream;
He gives Him all his best to savor
In wood and hill and field and stream.

The rosy dawn can never thrill them,
Those lazy souls who lie abed.
Their lives? Why, rocking cradles fill them,
And troubles, cares, and need for bread.

The brooks go leaping down the mountain,
The larks whir high to show their art;
Why can't my song burst from the fountain
Of my full throat and happy heart?

The ruling power, to God reserve it;
The brook, the lark, the field, the wood,
The earth, the sky, He will preserve it,
And guide my life to make it good.

Stewart H. Benedict

DER EINSIEDLER

Komm, Trost der Welt, du stille Nacht!
Wie steigst du von den Bergen sacht,
Die Lüfte alle schlafen.
Ein Schiffer nur noch, wandermüd,
Singt übers Meer sein Abendlied
Zu Gottes Lob im Hafen.

Die Jahre wie die Wolken gehn
Und lassen mich hier einsam stehn,
Die Welt hat mich vergessen,
Da tratst du wunderbar zu mir,
Wenn ich beim Waldesrauschen hier
Gedankenvoll gesessen.

O Trost der Welt, du stille Nacht!
Der Tag hat mich so müd gemacht,
Das weite Meer schon dunkelt,
Laß ausruhn mich von Lust und Not,
Bis daß das ew'ge Morgenrot
Den stillen Wald durchfunkelt.

THE HERMIT

Balm of the world, come, quiet night!
Thou sinkest from the mountains' height,
The evening winds are sleeping.
A sailor only, travel-worn,
Sings cross the port alone, forlorn,
His praise for God's safekeeping.

Like drifting clouds the years roll by.
Forgotten by the world stand I
Alone in all creation.
But oft thy comfort came to me
When underneath a rustling tree
I sat in contemplation.

Balm of the world, thou quiet night!
I'm wearied by the day's great might,
The wide, wide sea is darkling,
Grant me to rest from joy and woe
Till the eternal morning glow
Sets the dark forest sparkling.

Meno Spann

MONDNACHT

Es war, als hätt der Himmel
Die Erde still geküßt,
Daß sie im Blütenschimmer
Von ihm nun träumen müßt.

Die Luft ging durch die Felder,
Die Ähren wogten sacht,
Es rauschten leis die Wälder,
So sternklar war die Nacht.

Und meine Seele spannte
Weit ihre Flügel aus,
Flog durch die stillen Lande,
Als flöge sie nach Haus.

MOONLIT NIGHT

The sky had kissed the earth to sleep
So silently, 'twould seem,
That in her flowering glory she
Of him alone would dream.

Across the fields the playful breeze
The corn ears softly swayed,
A gentle whisper stirred the trees,
The night for stars was made.

My soul stretched out its yearning wings,
As far and wide to roam,
Flew through the quiet countryside,
As though 'twere flying home.

D. G. Wright

DIE NACHTBLUME

Nacht ist wie ein stilles Meer,
Lust und Leid und Liebesklagen
Kommen so verworren her
In dem linden Wellenschlagen.

Wünsche wie die Wolken sind,
Schiffen durch die stillen Räume,
Wer erkennt im lauen Wind,
Obs Gedanken oder Träume? –

Schließ ich nun auch Herz und Mund,
Die so gern den Sternen klagen:
Leise doch im Herzensgrund
Bleibt das linde Wellenschlagen.

NIGHT

Night is like a silent sea,
Joy and pain and love's sad urging
Reach us so confusedly
Through the gentle wavelet's surging.

Wishes like light clouds afloat,
Through the quiet spaces drifting,
In this soft wind who can note
If they're thoughts or dream-wraiths shifting?

If I silence voice and heart,
Which would cry out vainly urging
To the stars, still deep apart
Sounds that gentle wavelets' surging.

Isabel S. MacInnes

WÜNSCHELRUTE

Schläft ein Lied in allen Dingen,
Die da träumen fort und fort,
Und die Welt hebt an zu singen,
Triffst du nur das Zauberwort.

WISHING WAND

Slumb'ring deep in every thing
Dreams a song as yet unheard,
And the world begins to sing
If you find the magic word.

Alison Turner

Unbekannter Dichter

Schlaf', Kindlein, schlaf'!
Der Vater hüt't die Schaf',
Die Mutter schüttelt das Bäumelein,
Da fällt herab ein Träumelein.
Schlaf', Kindlein, schlaf'!

Schlaf', Kindlein, schlaf'!
Am Himmel ziehn die Schaf';
Die Sternlein sind die Lämmerlein,
Der Mond, der ist das Schäferlein.
Schlaf', Kindlein, schlaf'!

Schlaf', Kindlein, schlaf'!
So schenk ich dir ein Schaf
Mit einer goldnen Schelle fein,
Das soll dein Spielgeselle sein.
Schlaf', Kindlein, schlaf'!

Sleep, baby, sleep!
Thy father's tending sheep.
Thy mother shakes a little tree,
And down there falls a dream to thee.
Sleep, baby, sleep!

Sleep, baby, sleep!
Above pass by the sheep.
The stars are little lambs and soon
Will lead them on the shepherd moon.
Sleep, baby, sleep!

Sleep, baby, sleep!
Go 'way and guard the sheep!
Go 'way and watch, black shepherd pup,
And do not wake my baby up!
Sleep, baby, sleep!

Francis Owen

Wilhelm Müller

WANDERSCHAFT

Das Wandern ist des Müllers Lust,
Das Wandern!
Das muß ein schlechter Müller sein,
Dem niemals fiel das Wandern ein,
Das Wandern!

Vom Wasser haben wir's gelernt,
Vom Wasser!
Das hat nicht Rast bei Tag und Nacht,
Ist stets auf Wanderschaft bedacht,
Das Wasser!

Das sehn wir auch den Rädern ab,
Den Rädern!
Die gar nicht gerne stille stehn,
Die sich mein Tag nicht müde drehn.
Die Räder!

Die Steine selbst, so schwer sie sind,
Die Steine!
Sie tanzen mit den muntern Reihn
Und wollen gar noch schneller sein,
Die Steine!

O Wandern, Wandern, meine Lust,
O Wandern!
Herr Meister und Frau Meisterin,
Laßt mich in Friede weiter ziehn
Und wandern!

THE JOURNEYMAN'S SONG

Oh wandering is a miller's joy,
Oh wandering!
He must a sorry miller be
Who never wanted to be free
For wandering!

The water taught us what to do,
The water!
For it rests not by night or day,
And always strains to be away,
The water!

We learn it from the millwheels too,
The millwheels!
They're like the water down below,
I've never seen them weary grow,
The millwheels!

The millstones too, though heavy they,
The millstones!
In merry circles round they dance,
Would like to faster race and prance,
The millstones!

Oh wandering, wandering, my delight,
Oh wandering!
Oh master, mistress Miller, pray
Let me in peace now go away
And wander!

Francis Owen

DER LINDENBAUM

Am Brunnen vor dem Tore
Da steht ein Lindenbaum:
Ich träumt in seinem Schatten
So manchen süßen Traum.
Ich schnitt in seine Rinde
So manches liebe Wort;
Es zog in Freud und Leide
Zu ihm mich immer fort.

Ich mußt auch heute wandern
Vorbei in tiefer Nacht,
Da hab ich noch im Dunkel
Die Augen zugemacht.
Und seine Zweige rauschten,
Als riefen sie mir zu:
Komm her zu mir, Geselle,
Hier findst du deine Ruh!

Die kalten Winde bliesen
Mir grad ins Angesicht,
Der Hut flog mir vom Kopfe
Ich wendete mich nicht.
Nun bin ich manche Stunde
Entfernt von jenem Ort,
Und immer hör ichs rauschen:
Du fändest Ruhe dort!

AT THE FOUNTAIN BY THE GATEWAY

At fountain by the gateway
A lime tree's standing there;
I've dreamt within its shadow
Full many a dream so fair;
I've cut into its surface
Full many a loving word;
In joy and sorrow ever
Its call to me I've heard.

And still today in passing
At dead of night along,
I closed my eyes and listened
Those memories among;
And I could hear the branches,
As if they called to me:
Come back to me, old comrade,
And from your grief be free!

The chilling winds were blowing
Direct into my face;
My hat flew off and vanished,
I did not leave the place.
And now full many an hour
Away from that lime tree,
I hear it ever rustling:
You would have here been free!

Francis Owen

Annette von Droste-Hülshoff

DURCHWACHTE NACHT

Wie sank die Sonne glüh und schwer,
Und aus versengter Welle dann
Wie wirbelte der Nebel Heer
Die sternenlose Nacht heran! –
Ich höre ferne Schritte gehn –
Die Uhr schlägt zehn.

Noch ist nicht alles Leben eingenickt,
Der Schlafgemächer letzte Türen knarren;
Vorsichtig, in der Rinne Bauch gedrückt,
Schlüpft noch der Iltis an des Giebels Sparren,
Die schlummertrunkne Färse murrend nickt,
Und fern im Stalle dröhnt des Rosses Scharren,
Sein müdes Schnauben, bis, vom Mohn getränkt,
Sich schlaff die regungslose Flanke senkt.

Betäubend gleitet Fliederhauch
Durch meines Fensters offnen Spalt,
Und an der Scheibe grauem Rauch
Der Zweige wimmelnd Neigen wallt.
Matt bin ich, matt wie die Natur! –
Elf schlägt die Uhr.

O wunderliches Schlummerwachen, bist
Der zartren Nerve Fluch du oder Segen? –
's Ist eine Nacht vom Taue wach geküßt,
Das Dunkel fühl ich kühl wie feinen Regen
An meine Wangen gleiten, das Gerüst

WAKEFUL NIGHT

The sun went down with heavy glow
And from the flame-licked waters then
The swirling cohorts of the fog
Wheeled in the star-void empty night.
Receding footbeats far away –
The stroke of ten.

Some living creatures have not yet dozed off,
The latest bedroom doors are creaking shut;
And, crouched below the rain-trough's rim,
The fitchet slips around the gable ends;
The sleep-drunk nodding heifer softly lows
And from the stable the reverberant scrape
Of horse's hoof, a heaving weary sigh,
Then, drugged by sleep, the immobile flanks subside.

The lilac's heavy perfume drifts
From half-closed casements through my room,
Beyond the smoke-veil of the panes
The undulating branches throng.
I'm spent, as spent as nature is!
Eleven, the clock.

Ambiguous dozing sleeplessness, are you
The curse or solace of nerves finer spun?
The dew has kissed the night to wakefulness.
I feel the darkness cool as subtle rain
Brushing along my cheek; the frame on which

Des Vorhangs scheint sich schaukelnd zu bewegen,
Und dort das Wappen an der Decke Gips
Schwimmt sachte mit dem Schlängeln des Polyps.

Wie mir das Blut im Hirne zuckt!
Am Söller geht Geknister um,
Im Pulte raschelt es und ruckt,
Als drehe sich der Schlüssel um.
Und – horch! der Seiger hat gewacht!
's Ist Mitternacht.

War das ein Geisterlaut? So schwach und leicht
Wie kaum berührten Glases schwirrend Klingen
Und wieder wie verhaltnes Weinen steigt
Ein langer Klageton aus den Syringen,
Gedämpfter, süßer nun, wie tränenfeucht,
Und selig kämpft verschämter Liebe Ringen; –
O Nachtigall, das ist kein wacher Sang,
Ist nur im Traum gelöster Seele Drang.

Da kollerts nieder vom Gestein!
Des Turmes morsche Trümmer fällt,
Das Käuzlein knackt und hustet drein;
Ein jäher Windesodem schwellt
Gezweig und Kronenschmuck des Hains; –
Die Uhr schlägt eins.

Und drunten das Gewölke rollt und klimmt;
Gleich einer Lampe aus dem Hünenmale
Hervor des Mondes Silbergondel schwimmt,
Verzitternd auf der Gasse blauem Stahle;
An jedem Fliederblatt ein Fünkchen glimmt,
Und hell gezeichnet von dem blassen Strahle,
Legt auf mein Lager sich des Fensters Bild,
Vom schwanken Laubgewimmel überhüllt.

The curtains hang appears to sway and move,
The armorial bearings on the ceiling waver
With the serpentine pulsation of a squid.

A throb of blood within my brain!
Phantasmal footsteps creak about the loft,
Then rustling at the desk, a click
As though the key were being turned,
And – hark, the clock has stayed awake –
And midnight strikes!

Was that a spirit-noise? When scarcely brushed
A goblet's fading chime is not more faint;
Again like sobs suppressed there breaks from out
The lilacs long continued lamentation.
More muffled, sweeter, as if wet with tears,
Love struggles in a shamefast ecstasy –
O Nightingale, that is no waking song,
But pulsing of a dream-disprisoned soul.

A clicking slide of stone-work chips!
The ruined tower's crumbling down,
While screech owl snaps his beak and coughs;
A sudden puff of wind flings up
The boughs and treetops in the grove.
The clock strikes one.

Far, far below the cloud rack rolls and climbs;
And like a lamp from out a monstrous cairn
The moon glides on, a silver gondola,
A-tremble on its pathway's steely blue;
On every lilac leaf a droplet gleams,
And sharply outlined by the pallid light
The window-image falls upon my bed,
The swaying leafy tangle masking it.

Jetzt möcht ich schlafen, schlafen gleich,
Entschlafen unterm Mondeshauch,
Umspielt vom flüsternden Gezweig,
Im Blute Funken, Funk im Strauch,
Und mir im Ohre Melodei; –
Die Uhr schlägt zwei.

Und immer heller wird der süße Klang,
Das liebe Lachen; es beginnt zu ziehen
Gleich Bildern von Daguerre die Deck entlang,
Die aufwärts steigen mit des Pfeiles Fliehen;
Mir ist, als seh ich lichter Locken Hang,
Gleich Feuerwürmern seh ich Augen glühen,
Dann werden feucht sie, werden blau und lind,
Und mir zu Füßen sitzt ein schönes Kind.

Es sieht empor, so froh gespannt,
Die Seele strömend aus dem Blick;
Nun hebt es gaukelnd seine Hand,
Nun zieht es lachend sie zurück;
Und – horch! des Hahnes erster Schrei! –
Die Uhr schlägt drei.

Wie bin ich aufgeschreckt, – o süßes Bild,
Du bist dahin, zerflossen mit dem Dunkel!
Die unerfreulich graue Dämmrung quillt,
Verloschen ist des Flieders Taugefunkel,
Verrostet steht des Mondes Silberschild,
Im Walde gleitet ängstliches Gemunkel,
Und meine Schwalbe an des Frieses Saum
Zirpt leise, leise auf im schweren Traum.

Der Tauben Schwärme kreisen scheu,
Wie trunken in des Hofes Rund,
Und wieder gellt des Hahnes Schrei,

Why can't I sleep, drop off at once
And in the moon-haze drift to sleep
Enveloped by the whisper of the boughs,
Flame-points within me, on the leaves,
And in my ears a melody; –
The clock strikes two.

And ever brighter grows the lovely sound,
Delightful laughter, there begin to move
Along the ceiling pictures like Daguerre's
Ascending swiftly like an arrow's flight;
I seem to see cascading yellow locks
And now I see the glowworm gleam of eyes
Which next become a moist and gentle blue
And at my feet there sits a lovely child.

It lifts its lids and from its eyes
The soul's expectant joy pours out;
It waves a teasing dainty hand
And then, all laughing, pulls it back.
And – listen! That's the cock's first cry!
The clock strikes three.

That startled me! – O lovely image, are
You gone, quite dissipated with the dark?
The gray, depressing half-light spreads,
The dewey sparkle of the lilac's gone,
The silver moon-shield's lost its burnished gleam,
And trepid rumors float throughout the woods;
My swallow, perching on the frieze's edge,
Chirps faintly, faintly, from the depths of dreams.

In wary rounds the pigeons fly,
Befuddled, in the courtyard square,
And once again the cock crows shrill;

Auf seiner Streue rückt der Hund,
Und langsam knarrt des Stalles Tür –
Die Uhr schlägt vier.

Da flammts im Osten auf, – o Morgenglut!
Sie steigt, sie steigt, und mit dem ersten Strahle
Strömt Wald und Heide vor Gesangesflut,
Das Leben quillt aus schäumendem Pokale,
Es klirrt die Sense, flattert Falkenbrut,
Im nahen Forste schmettern Jagdsignale,
Und wie ein Gletscher sinkt der Träume Land
Zerrinnend in des Horizontes Brand.

The watchdog twitches on his straw,
The stall-door slowly creaks ajar –
The clock strikes four.

There flares the eastern sky – the morning glow!
It climbs, it rises: with the earliest ray
Freshets of song stream over wood and moor
And life spills over from a bubbling cup.
The scythes commence to twang, the hawk-tribes soar,
The forest fills with blaring hunting horns,
And glacierlike, my land of dreams subsides,
Disintegrates as the horizon flames.

                                        S. G. Flygt

IM GRASE

Süße Ruh, süßer Taumel im Gras,
Von des Krautes Arome umhaucht,
Tiefe Flut, tief tief trunkne Flut,
Wenn die Wolk am Azure verraucht,
Wenn aufs müde, schwimmende Haupt
Süßes Lachen gaukelt herab,
Liebe Stimme säuselt und träuft
Wie die Lindenblüt auf ein Grab.

Wenn im Busen die Toten dann,
Jede Leiche sich streckt und regt,
Leise, leise den Odem zieht,
Die geschloßne Wimper bewegt,
Tote Lieb, tote Lust, tote Zeit,
All die Schätze, im Schutt verwühlt,
Sich berühren mit schüchternem Klang
Gleich den Glöckchen, vom Winde umspielt.

Stunden, flücht'ger ihr als der Kuß
Eines Strahls auf den trauernden See,
Als des ziehenden Vogels Lied,
Das mir niederperlt aus der Höh,
Als des schillernden Käfers Blitz,
Wenn den Sonnenpfad er durcheilt,
Als der heiße Druck einer Hand,
Die zum letzten Male verweilt.

Dennoch, Himmel, immer mir nur
Dieses eine: nur für das Lied
Jedes freien Vogels im Blau
Eine Seele, die mit ihm zieht,
Nur für jeden kärglichen Strahl
Meinen farbigschillernden Saum,
Jeder warmen Hand meinen Druck,
Und für jedes Glück meinen Traum.

IN THE GRASS

Sweet repose, oh tumult sweet in the grass,
Caressed by the fragrance of herbs,
Deep the surge, deep, deep drunken the surge,
When the clouds wisp away from the blue,
And sweet laughter comes flickering down
On my whirling, languorous head,
Precious voice, susurrant of balm,
Like linden-bloom on a grave.

When the Dead in my bosom then,
Every mummy stretches and stirs,
Softly, softly drawing its breath,
Fluttering tight-closed lids,
Dead love, dead time and dead joy,
All my treasures, interred in the dust,
Start to pulsate with diffident chime
Like bells that the wind has caressed.

O hours more fleet than the kiss
Of the sun on the sorrowing lake,
Than the song of the wide-faring bird
Bubbling down to my ears from the sky,
Than the beetle's glistering flash
Cutting the sunlight-shaft,
Than the fleeting touch of a hand
That will never be felt again.

Still, O Heaven, grant only this,
Only this, and no more: for the song
Of each free-winging bird in the sky
A wide-faring soul that follows;
For each scanty pencil of light
My fringe of shimmering hues;
For ev'ry warm hand-clasp my own,
And for every joy, but a dream.

S. G. Flygt

Heinrich Heine

Leise zieht durch mein Gemüt
Liebliches Geläute,
Klinge, kleines Frühlingslied,
Kling' hinaus ins Weite.

Kling' hinaus bis an das Haus,
Wo die Blumen sprießen.
Wenn du eine Rose schaust,
Sag' ich lass' sie grüßen.

Softly through my spirit flow
Melodies entreating;
Fill the air with songs and go,
Bear my springtime greeting.

Sing my lay where flowers gay
Deck a house you're meeting;
If you see a rose that way,
Say, I send her greeting.

Francis Owen

Ein Jüngling liebt ein Mädchen,
Die hat einen andern erwählt;
Der andre liebt eine andre,
Und hat sich mit dieser vermählt.

Das Mädchen heiratet aus Ärger
Den ersten besten Mann,
Der ihr in den Weg gelaufen;
Der Jüngling ist übel dran.

Es ist eine alte Geschichte,
Doch bleibt sie immer neu;
Und wem sie just passieret,
Dem bricht das Herz entzwei.

A young man loves a maiden,
Who loves another youth;
This other loves another,
To whom he's wed, in truth.

The maiden marries in anger
The first that comes along
By chance to cross her pathway;
The young man feels this wrong.

It is an age-old story,
And yet it's always new;
The heart, to whom this happens,
Will surely split in two.

D. G. Wright

Es war ein alter König,
Sein Herz war schwer, sein Haupt war grau;
Der arme, alte König,
Er nahm eine junge Frau.

Es war ein schöner Page,
Blond war sein Haupt, leicht war sein Sinn;
Er trug die seidne Schleppe
Der jungen Königin.

Kennst du das alte Liedchen?
Es klingt so süß, es klingt so trüb!
Sie mußten beide sterben,
Sie hatten sich viel zu lieb.

There was an aged monarch,
His heart was grave, his hair was gray;
This poor old monarch married
A maid that was young and gay.

There was a handsome page-boy,
Blond was his hair, bright was his mien;
He bore the silken train
Of this so youthful queen.

You know this old, old story?
It sounds so sweet, so sad to tell!
The lovers had to perish,
They loved each other too well.

Karl Weimar

Die Lotusblume ängstigt
Sich vor der Sonne Pracht,
Und mit gesenktem Haupte
Erwartet sie träumend die Nacht.

Der Mond, der ist ihr Buhle,
Er weckt sie mit seinem Licht,
Und ihm entschleiert sie freundlich
Ihr frommes Blumengesicht.

Sie blüht und glüht und leuchtet,
Und starret stumm in die Höh;
Sie duftet und weinet und zittert
Vor Liebe und Liebesweh.

The lotus-flower is frightened
By the sunshine's brilliant light,
With drooping head, and dreaming,
She waits the fall of night.

The moon, who is her lover,
Wakes her with shining grace,
And she unveils so gladly
Her gentle flowering face.

She blooms and glows and glimmers,
Stares up to the starry main;
Fragrant, she weeps and trembles
With love and love's sweet pain.

D. G. Wright

Du sollst mich liebend umschließen,
Geliebtes, schönes Weib!
Umschling mich mit Armen und Füßen
Und mit dem geschmeidigen Leib.

Gewaltig hat umfangen
Umwunden, umschlungen schon
Die allerschönste der Schlangen
Den glücklichsten Laokoon.

My beautiful love, keep bound me
As only you can do.
Wrap your hands and your feet around me
And your agile body too.

And now in mighty embraces
Entwining and holding on
The most beautiful serpent faces
The happiest Laocoon.

Meno Spann

Ein Fichtenbaum steht einsam
Im Norden auf kahler Höh.
Ihn schläfert; mit weißer Decke
Umhüllen ihn Eis und Schnee.

Er träumt von einer Palme,
Die, fern im Morgenland,
Einsam und schweigend trauert
Auf brennender Felsenwand.

A fir tree standing lonely
On a windswept northern height
Slumbered under the icy
Covering of white;

Slumbered and dreamed of a palm tree
Far in an Orient land,
Lonely and silent mourning
On a cliff of burning sand.

Margaret R. Richter

WO?

Wo wird einst des Wandermüden
Letzte Ruhestätte sein?
Unter Palmen in dem Süden?
Unter Linden an dem Rhein?

Werd' ich wo in einer Wüste
Eingescharrt von fremder Hand?
Oder ruh' ich an der Küste
Eines Meeres in dem Sand?

Immerhin! Mich wird umgeben
Gotteshimmel, dort wie hier,
Und als Totenlampen schweben
Nachts die Sterne über mir.

WHERE?

What last resting place awaits me
When this weary journey's done?
By the Rhine, beneath the lime trees?
Under palms and southern sun?

Will some stranger's hand inter me
In the desert's shifting sand?
Shall I rest beside the ocean
On some seacoast's salty strand?

Yet God's sky will be above me
Still, no matter where I lie.
And at night the stars will hang there,
Funeral candles in the sky.

Helen Sebba

Ich hatte einst ein schönes Vaterland.
Der Eichenbaum
Wuchs dort so hoch, die Veilchen nickten sanft,
Es war ein Traum.

Das küßte mich auf deutsch und sprach auf deutsch
(Man glaubt es kaum
Wie gut es klang) das Wort: ,,Ich liebe dich!"
Es war ein Traum.

I used to have the fairest fatherland.
The oak trees there
Were tall, so tall; the violets soft and blue.
A dream — so fair.

The kisses were in German and the word —
Strange though it seem,
It rang so true — the word: Ich liebe dich.
A dream, a dream.

Alexander Gode

Friedrich Hauff

REITERS MORGENGESANG

Morgenrot,
Leuchtest mir zum frühen Tod?
Bald wird die Trompete blasen,
Dann muß ich mein Leben lassen,
Ich und mancher Kamerad.

Kaum gedacht,
Ward der Lust ein End gemacht!
Gestern noch auf stolzen Rossen,
Heute durch die Brust geschossen,
Morgen in das kühle Grab.

Ach, wie bald
Schwindet Schönheit und Gestalt!
Prahlst du gleich mit deinen Wangen,
Die wie Milch und Purpur prangen?
Ach, die Rosen welken all!

Darum still
Füg ich mich, wie Gott es will.
Nun, so will ich wacker streiten
Und sollt ich den Tod erleiden,
Stirbt ein wackrer Reitersmann.

TO A DUTCH LANDSCAPE

Weary is the brooklet's flow,
Here is heard no wand'ring breeze;
Leaves fall softly from the trees,
Tired and pale, to earth below.

Crows, whose wings move but a trace,
Fly so slowly; on the hill
Windmill arms are resting, still,
Oh, how sleepy is this place!

Spring and summer have flown by;
There the hut, as if in spite,
Has its straw hat, shunning light,
Drawn down far below its eye.

Dozing through the idle days,
Lies the shepherd by his sheep.
Nature, spinning autumn haze,
Now has found forgetful sleep.

Roger C. Norton

SCHILFLIED (V)

Auf dem Teich, dem regungslosen,
Weilt des Mondes holder Glanz,
Flechtend seine bleichen Rosen
In des Schilfes grünen Kranz.

Hirsche wandeln dort am Hügel,
Blicken in die Nacht empor;
Manchmal regt sich das Geflügel
Träumerisch im tiefen Rohr.

Weinend muß mein Blick sich senken;
Durch die tiefste Seele geht
Mir ein süßes Deingedenken
Wie ein stilles Nachtgebet!

SONG OF THE RUSHES (V)

On the pond, which now reposes,
Moonbeams in full beauty glow,
As they plait their pallid roses
Where green wreaths of rushes grow.

On the hill the deer are roaming,
Looking upward into night;
In the rushes' restful gloaming,
Birds stir oft with dream's delight.

Tearfully my glance is falling;
Through my deepest soul's dark lair
Thoughts of you come sweetly calling
Like a quiet evening prayer.

                              Roger C. Norton

DIE DREI ZIGEUNER

Drei Zigeuner fand ich einmal
Liegen an einer Weide,
Als mein Fuhrwerk mit müder Qual
Schlich durch sandige Heide.

Hielt der eine für sich allein
In den Händen die Fiedel,
Spielte, umglüht vom Abendschein,
Sich ein feuriges Liedel.

Hielt der zweite die Pfeif im Mund,
Blickte nach seinem Rauche,
Froh, als ob er vom Erdenrund
Nichts zum Glücke mehr brauche.

Und der dritte behaglich schlief,
Und sein Zimbal am Baum hing,
Über die Saiten ein Windhauch lief,
Über sein Herz ein Traum ging.

An den Kleidern trugen die drei
Löcher und bunte Flicken;
Aber sie boten trotzig frei
Spott den Erdengeschicken.

Dreifach haben sie mir gezeigt,
Wenn das Leben uns nachtet,
Wie mans verraucht, verschläft, vergeigt
Und es dreimal verachtet.

Nach den Zigeunern lang noch schaun
Mußt ich im Weiterfahren,
Nach den Gesichtern dunkelbraun,
Den schwarzlockigen Haaren.

THE THREE GYPSIES

Gypsies three I found one day,
'Gainst a willow lying,
As my coach its cumbrous way
Through the heath was plying.

One of the three a fiddle bowed
For his own sweet pleasure;
While the sunset round him glowed,
Played he a fiery measure.

And the second with many a puff
Watched the smoke rings vanish,
Looking as though a pipe were enough
Cares from life to banish.

And the third one calmly slept;
From his cimbal a gleam glanced;
Over its strings the wind's breath swept,
Over his heart a dream danced.

Stains and patches their garments displayed,
Which were rent and tattered,
But their defiant looks conveyed
That only freedom mattered.

Threefold they showed me how to be gay
When by life we are daunted,
How to fiddle, smoke, sleep it away,
How it may three times be taunted.

Back at the gypsies long I gazed
From my coach's traces,
At their black locks, sunset-glazed,
At their dark brown faces.

Gerd Gillhoff

DIE DREI

Drei Reiter nach verlorner Schlacht,
Wie reiten sie so sacht, so sacht!

Aus tiefen Wunden quillt das Blut,
Es spürt das Roß die warme Flut.

Vom Sattel tropft das Blut, vom Zaun,
Und spült hinunter Staub und Schaum.

Die Rosse schreiten sanft und weich,
Sonst flöß' das Blut zu rasch, zu reich.

Die Reiter reiten dicht gesellt,
Und einer sich am andern hält.

Sie sehn sich traurig ins Gesicht,
Und einer um den andern spricht:

„Mir blüht daheim die schönste Maid,
Drum tut mein früher Tod mir leid."

„Hab' Haus und Hof und grünen Wald,
Und sterben muß ich hier so bald!"

„Den Blick hab' ich in Gottes Welt,
Sonst nichts, doch schwer mir's Sterben fällt."

Und lauernd auf den Todesritt
Ziehn durch die Luft drei Geier mit.

Sie teilen kreischend unter sich:
„Den speisest du, den du, den ich."

THE THREE

Three riders after harsh defeat,
How slowly, slowly they retreat!

From deep-cut gashes flows their blood,
The horses feel the tepid flood.

From saddle drips the blood, from rein,
And washes dust off flank and mane.

The steed's advance is gently slow,
Or else too swift the blood's rich flow.

The dying horsemen, side by side,
Clasp one another while they ride,

And each with mien disconsolate
Now mourns that this should be his fate:

"A maid has promised me her hand –
Why must I die in foreign land?"

"Have home and farm and forest green,
And meet a death so unforeseen!"

"God gave me life, his only boon,
And yet I dread to die so soon."

And where they on their death-ride fare,
Three vultures follow through the air.

They share the men with piercing cry:
"Him you devour, him you, him I!"

Gerd Gillhoff

BITTE

Weil auf mir, du dunkles Auge,
Übe deine ganze Macht,
Ernste, milde, träumerische,
Unergründlich süße Nacht!

Nimm mit deinem Zauberdunkel
Diese Welt von hinnen mir,
Daß du über meinem Leben
Einsam schwebest für und für.

PLEA

Rest upon me, eye of darkness,
Practice now your every might,
Never fathomed in your beauty,
Solemn, gentle, dreaming night.

By the magic of your darkness
Take from me this world away,
That above my life forever
Lonely you may keep your sway.

George C. Schoolfield

Julius Mosen

DER TRÄUMENDE SEE

Der See ruht tief im blauen Traum,
Von Wasserblumen zugedeckt;
Ihr Vöglein hoch im Fichtenbaum,
Daß ihr mir nicht den Schläfer weckt!

Doch leise weht das Schilf und wiegt
Das Haupt mit leichtem Sinn;
Ein blauer Falter aber fliegt
Darüber einsam hin!

THE DREAMING LAKE

The lake, in dark-blue reverie,
Sleeps 'neath a quilt of water flowers.
You small birds, in your spruce-tree home,
Do not disturb the placid hours.

The sedge waves softly, nods its head,
Light-hearted, free from care;
A glowing turquoise butterfly
Soars, lonely, through the air.

Anne Jennings

Eduard Möricke

SCHÖN-ROHTRAUT

Wie heißt König Ringangs Töchterlein?
Rohtraut, Schön-Rohtraut.
Was tut sie denn den ganzen Tag,
Da sie wohl nicht spinnen und nähen mag?
Tut fischen und jagen.
O daß ich doch ihr Jäger wär!
Fischen und Jagen freute mich sehr.
– Schweig stille, mein Herze!

Und über eine kleine Weil,
Rohtraut, Schön-Rohtraut,
So dient der Knab auf Ringangs Schloß
In Jägertracht und hat ein Roß,
Mit Rohtraut zu jagen.
O daß ich doch ein Königssohn wär!
Rohtraut, Schön-Rohtraut lieb ich so sehr.
– Schweig stille, mein Herze!

Einsmals sie ruhten am Eichenbaum,
Da lacht Schön-Rohtraut:
„Was siehst mich an so wunniglich?
Wenn du das Herz hast, küsse mich!"
Ach! erschrak der Knabe!
Doch denket er: „Mir ist's vergunnt",
Und küsset Schön-Rohtraut auf den Mund.
– Schweig stille, mein Herze!

Darauf sie ritten schweigend heim,
Rohtraut, Schön-Rohtraut;
Es jauchzt der Knab in seinem Sinn!

FAIR ROHTRAUT

Oh, what is the name of King Ringang's daughter?
Rohtraut, Fair Rohtraut.
And what does she do the live-long day,
Since she scarcely would spin and knit alway?
She goes fishing and hunting.
Oh, that her huntsman I might be!
I'd fish and hunt right merrily.
– Ah, be silent, my heart!

And after just a little while,
Rohtraut, Fair Rohtraut,
The lad did serve at Ringang's court
In squire's garb and had a horse,
To hunt with Rohtraut.
Oh, that a king's son I might be!
I love Fair Rohtraut tenderly.
– Ah, be silent, my heart!

One day they stopped by an old oak tree,
Then laughed Fair Rohtraut:
"Why look at me so blissfully?
If you have courage, come, kiss me!"
Oh, how startled the lad was!
And yet he thinks: 'Twas offered me,"
And kisses Fair Rohtraut tenderly.
– Ah, be silent, my heart!

And then they rode quite silent home,
Rohtraut, Fair Rohtraut;
The lad exulted all the way:

„Und würdst du heute Kaiserin,
Mich sollt's nicht kränken !
Ihr tausend Blätter im Walde wißt,
Ich hab Schön-Rohtrauts Mund geküßt !
– Schweig stille, mein Herze!"

Though you were made an Empress today,
It would not grieve me;
Ye thousand leaves in the forest, hear!
I've kissed Fair Rohtraut's mouth so dear!
Ah, be silent, my heart!

Isabel S. MacInnes

DER GÄRTNER

Auf ihrem Leibrößlein,
So weiß wie der Schnee,
Die schönste Prinzessin
Reit't durch die Allee.

Der Weg, den das Rößlein
Hintanzet so hold,
Der Sand, den ich streute,
Er blinket wie Gold.

Du rosenfarbs Hütlein,
Wohl auf und wohl ab,
O wirf eine Feder
Verstohlen herab!

Und willst du dagegen
Eine Blüte von mir,
Nimm tausend für eine,
Nimm alle dafür!

THE GARDENER

On her fleet little charger
As white as the snow
The handsomest princess
Rides through the park row.

The path which the horse strides
So gay and so bold,
The sand that I scattered,
It sparkles like gold.

You pink-colored bonnet,
Now up and now down,
Oh throw me a feather
Clandestinely down!

And should you desire
A flower today,
Take a thousand in barter,
Take a fulsome bouquet!

Ernst Rose

EIN STÜNDLEIN WOHL VOR TAG

Derweil ich schlafend lag,
Ein Stündlein wohl vor Tag,
Sang vor dem Fenster auf dem Baum
Ein Schwälblein mir, ich hört' es kaum,
Ein Stündlein wohl vor Tag:

„Hör' an, was ich dir sag',
Dein Schätzlein ich verklag':
Derweil ich dieses singen tu',
Herzt er ein Lieb in guter Ruh',
Ein Stündlein wohl vor Tag."

O weh! nichts weiter sag!
O still! nichts hören mag!
Flieg ab! flieg ab von meinem Baum!
– Ach, Lieb' und Treu' ist wie ein Traum
Ein Stündlein wohl vor Tag.

AN HOUR BEFORE THE DAY

The while I sleeping lay,
An hour before the day,
Outside my window sang a bird
So softly that I scarcely heard,
An hour before the day:

"Heed well what now I say!
False is your sweetheart's play.
The while I sing – it must be told –
His arms another maid enfold,
An hour before the day."

O woe! No more betray!
Hush, hush! Away, away!
Fly from my window, cruel bird!
O, faith is but a wistful word
An hour before the day!

Gerd Gillhoff

VERBORGENHEIT

Laß, o Welt, o laß mich sein!
Locket nicht mit Liebesgaben,
Laßt dies Herz alleine haben
Seine Wonne, seine Pein!

Was ich traure, weiß ich nicht,
Es ist unbekanntes Wehe;
Immerdar durch Tränen sehe
Ich der Sonne liebes Licht.

Oft bin ich mir kaum bewußt,
Und die helle Freude zücket
Durch die Schwere, so mich drücket,
Wonniglich in meiner Brust.

Laß, o Welt, o laß mich sein!
Locket nicht mit Liebesgaben,
Laßt dies Herz alleine haben
Seine Wonne, seine Pein!

SECLUSION

Leave me, world, just let me go!
Tempt me not with soothing pleasure,
Leave this heart alone to treasure
All its rapture, all its woe!

Why I grieve, I do not know:
Mine is unexplained lamenting;
Still through all my senseless weeping
I behold the sun's bright glow.

Oft I feel so far apart,
And a joyful gladness draws me
Through the troubles that oppress me
Blissfully within my heart.

Leave me, world, just let me go!
Tempt me not with soothing pleasure,
Leave this heart alone to treasure
All its rapture, all its woe!

D. G. Wright

DENK ES, O SEELE!

Ein Tännlein grünet wo,
Wer weiß, im Walde,
Ein Rosenstrauch, wer sagt,
In welchem Garten?
Sie sind erlesen schon,
Denk es, o Seele!
Auf deinem Grab zu wurzeln
Und zu wachsen.

Zwei schwarze Rößlein weiden,
Auf der Wiese,
Sie kehren heim zur Stadt
In muntern Sprüngen.
Sie werden schrittweis gehn
Mit deiner Leiche;
Vielleicht, vielleicht noch eh
An ihren Hufen
Das Eisen los wird,
Das ich blitzen sehe!

THINK OF IT, MY SOUL

Green stands a fir tree, who
Knows where in the forest, – –
A rosebush, who can tell
Within what garden?
They are already chosen –
Think of it, my soul –
To root themselves and grow
Upon thy grave.

Two jet-black horses pasture
On the meadow;
Home to town they come
Jauntily prancing.
At slow walk they will pace
Before thy corpse
Sooner perhaps . . . perhaps . . .
Than on their hooves
The shoe-iron loosens
Which I see flashing.

Charles E. Passage

Friedrich Hebbel

ICH UND DU

Wir träumten voneinander
Und sind davon erwacht,
Wir leben, um uns zu lieben,
Und sinken zurück in die Nacht.

Du tratst aus meinem Traume,
Aus deinem trat ich hervor,
Wir sterben, wenn sich Eines
Im Andern ganz verlor.

Auf einer Lilie zittern
Zwei Tropfen, rein und rund,
Zerfließen in Eins und rollen
Hinab in des Kelches Grund.

YOU AND I

We dreamed of one another
And wakened to the light;
We live to love each other
And sink back into the night.

You stepped out of my dreaming,
Out of your dream stepped I;
If either is ever wholly
Lost in the other, we die.

Upon a lily tremble
Two clear, round drops. They kiss,
Dissolve into one, and go rolling
Into the throat's abyss.

Calvin S. Brown

ADAMS OPFER

Die schönsten Früchte, frisch gepflückt,
Trägt er zum grünen Festaltar
Und bringt, mit Blumen reich geschmückt,
Sie fromm als Morgenopfer dar.

Erst blickt er froh, dann wird er still:
— O Herr, wie arm erschein' ich mir!
Wenn ich den Dank dir bringen will,
So borge ich selbst den von dir! —

ADAM'S OFFERING

The sweetest fruits, all freshly picked,
Unto the altar does he bear
And as a morning offering, decked
With flowers, devoutly lays them there.

Joyous at first, then hushed anew:
"Oh Lord, how poor I seem to me!
When I would bring Thee thanks, so do
I borrow even that from Thee!"

Lyn Goetze Snyder

DER BAUM IN DER WÜSTE

Es steht ein Baum im Wüstensand,
Der einzige, der dort gedieh;
Die Sonne hat ihn fast verbrannt,
Der Regen tränkt den durst'gen nie.

In seiner falben Krone hängt
Gewürzig eine Frucht voll Saft,
Er hat sein Mark hineingedrängt,
Sein Leben, seine höchste Kraft.

Die Stunde, wo sie überschwer
Zu Boden fallen muß, ist nah;
Es zieht kein Wanderer daher,
Und für ihn selbst ist sie nicht da.

THE TREE IN THE DESERT

In desert wastes there stands a tree,
The only one that there could thrive;
The sun has almost burnt it up,
No raindrops help it keep alive.

Amidst its faded leaves there hangs
A spicy fruit, full ripe and fair,
A fruit the tree has spent its life
And all its highest art to bear.

The moment nears. The heavy fruit
Must fall, it cannot linger on.
No wanderer comes near the tree.
It only knows the fruit is gone.

Frances Stillman

SOMMERBILD

Ich sah des Sommers letzte Rose stehn,
Sie war, als ob sie bluten könne, rot;
Da sprach ich schauernd im Vorübergehn:
So weit im Leben ist zu nah am Tod!

Es regte sich kein Hauch am heißen Tag,
Nur leise strich ein weißer Schmetterling;
Doch ob auch kaum die Luft sein Flügelschlag
Bewegte, sie empfand es und verging.

SUMMER IMAGE

The summer's last surviving rose I saw,
So crimson-hued as if it blood could shed.
Then, passing by, I said in doleful awe,
"So far in life is near the end we dread."

No breath of air stirred on that sultry day,
No being moved but one white butterfly;
Yet, though the air scarce felt its wings' light sway,
The red rose trembled, and I saw it die.

Gerd Gillhoff

HERBSTBILD

Dies ist ein Herbsttag, wie ich keinen sah!
Die Luft ist still, als atmete man kaum,
Und dennoch fallen raschelnd, fern und nah,
Die schönsten Früchte ab von jedem Baum.

O stört sie nicht, die Feier der Natur!
Dies ist die Lese, die sie selber hält,
Denn heute löst sich von den Zweigen nur,
Was vor dem milden Strahl der Sonne fällt.

PICTURE OF AUTUMN

This autumn day – I have not seen its peer.
The air so calm that loath to breathe seems all,
And yet, from every tree, both far and near,
Through rustling leaves the choicest fruits do fall.

Oh let no one disturb this harvest feast
Which Nature all alone enacts this day.
The fruits that fall are from their branch released
By gentle nudging of the sun's mild ray.

Alexander Gode

NACHTLIED

Quellende, schwellende Nacht,
Voll von Lichtern und Sternen;
In den ewigen Fernen,
Sage, was ist da erwacht?

Herz in der Brust wird beengt;
Steigendes, neigendes Leben,
Riesenhaft fühle ichs weben,
Welches das meine verdrängt.

Schlaf, da nahst du dich leis
Wie dem Kinde die Amme,
Und um die dürftige Flamme
Ziehst du den schützenden Kreis.

NIGHT

Urging, upsurging night,
Brimming with shimmer and star,
In the eternal afar,
Tell, what is coming to light?

Heart in the breast turns to stone;
Pendent, ascendent life,
I feel the vast web of its strife
As it displaces my own.

Gently thou comest now, sleep,
Like nurse to child, softly going
And 'round the flame's feeble glowing
Raisest the safeguarding keep.

Paul F. Guenther

Georg Herwegh

SHELLEY

Um seinen Gott sich doppelt schmerzlich mühend,
War er ihm, selbsterrungen, doppelt teuer,
Dem Ewigen war keine Seele treuer,
Kein Glaube je so ungeschwächt und blühend.

Mit allen Pulsen für die Menschheit glühend,
Saß immer mit der Hoffnung er am Steuer,
Wenn er auch zürnte, seines Zornes Feuer
Nur gegen Sklaven und Tyrannen sprühend.

Ein Elfengeist in einem Menschenleibe,
Von der Natur Altar ein reiner Funken,
Und drum für Englands Pöbelsinn die Scheibe;

Ein Herz, vom süßen Duft des Himmels trunken,
Verflucht vom Vater und geliebt vom Weibe,
Zuletzt ein Stern, im wilden Meer versunken.

SHELLEY

Through painful God-search, he, the doubly striving,
To Him, the self-found, doubly was endeared,
God was by none more loyally revered,
No faith was ever so confirmed and thriving.

Love of all men his every heartbeat driving,
He always full of hope his vessel steered,
The measure of his fury only geared
To slavery and tyrannous conniving.

A fairy spirit, by a human claimed,
Pure spark by nature's altar set in motion,
A target at which England's mob-minds aimed.

A heart, drunk with sweet heaven's fragrant potion,
Beloved by women, by his sire defamed,
At last a star, sunk in a savage ocean.

Paul F. Guenther

Theodor Storm

DIE STADT

Am grauen Strand, am grauen Meer
Und seitab liegt die Stadt;
Der Nebel drückt die Dächer schwer,
Und durch die Stille braust das Meer
Eintönig um die Stadt.

Es rauscht kein Wald, es schlägt im Mai
Kein Vogel ohn' Unterlaß;
Die Wandergans mit hartem Schrei
Nur fliegt in Herbstesnacht vorbei,
Am Strande weht das Gras.

Doch hängt mein ganzes Herz an dir,
Du graue Stadt am Meer;
Der Jugend Zauber für und für
Ruht lächelnd doch auf dir, auf dir,
Du graue Stadt am Meer.

THE TOWN

Gray is the sea; the shore is gray.
Behind it lies the town.
On roofs and sheds fog rests its spray.
Monotonously roars the bay
Around a quiet town.

No forest murmurs, and no sigh
Of birds is heard in May.
Wild geese in autumn nights fly by
And shriek their shrill, harsh, moaning cry.
Dry reeds in sand dunes play.

And yet, my heart belongs to you,
Gray city by the sea.
Enchantments of my youth endue
Forever smilingly just you,
Gray city by the sea.

R. N. Linn

JULI

Klingt im Wind ein Wiegenlied,
Sonne warm herniedersieht,
Seine Ähren senkt das Korn,
Rote Beere schwillt am Dorn,
Schwer von Segen ist die Flur –
Junge Frau, was sinnst du nur?

JULY

In the breeze a humming tune
Warming rays from sun at noon
Swaying rye field, ears bent low
Bursting berries in the sloe
Countryside with blessings fraught
What, young woman, fills your thought?

Alexander Gode

AUGUST-INSERAT

„Die verehrlichen Jungen, welche heuer
Meine Äpfel und Birnen zu stehlen gedenken,
Ersuche ich höflichst, bei diesem Vergnügen
Womöglich insoweit sich zu beschränken,
Daß sie daneben auf den Beeten
Mir die Wurzeln und Erbsen nicht zertreten."

AUGUST-ADVERTISEMENT

Of the honorable young gentlemen who this year
May be considering the theft of apples and pears that are mine
I respectfully request that during this amusement,
As far as it is possible they will themselves confine,
Not entering the beds nearby, please,
To avoid trampling down my plants and peas.

Frances Sturmer-Robb

Schließe mir die Augen beide
Mit den lieben Händen zu!
Geht doch alles, was ich leide,
Unter deiner Hand zur Ruh.

Und wie leise sich der Schmerz
Well' um Welle schlafen leget,
Wie der letzte Schlag sich reget,
Füllest du mein ganzes Herz.

Both my eyes, my dearest, close
With your loving hands, I pray!
All my sufferings, all my woes,
Neath your hands are smoothed away.

Softly as the pain is stilled,
Each successive wave abates,
As the final beat pulsates,
All my heart with you is filled.

D. G. Wright

TROST

So komme, was da kommen mag!
Solang du lebest, ist es Tag.

Und geht es in die Welt hinaus,
Wo du mir bist, bin ich zu Haus.

Ich seh dein liebes Angesicht,
Ich sehe die Schatten der Zukunft nicht.

CONSOLATION

Let come what will, let come what may!
So long you live, it is still day.

Wherever in the world I roam,
Where'er you are, for me is home.

I gaze upon your lovely face,
No shadows of the future trace.

D. G. Wright

Gottfried Keller

DIE ÖFFENTLICHEN VERLEUMDER

Ein Ungeziefer ruht
In Staub und trocknem Schlamme
Verborgen, wie die Flamme
In leichter Asche tut.
Ein Regen, Windeshauch
Erweckt das schlimme Leben,
Und aus dem Nichts erheben
Sich Seuchen, Glut und Rauch.

Aus dunkler Höhle fährt
Ein Schächer, um zu schweifen;
Nach Beuteln möcht' er greifen
Und findet bessern Wert:
Er findet einen Streit
Um nichts, ein irres Wissen,
Ein Banner, das zerrissen,
Ein Volk in Blödigkeit.

Er findet, wo er geht,
Die Leere dürft'ger Zeiten,
Da kann er schamlos schreiten,
Nun wird er ein Prophet;
Auf einen Kehricht stellt
Er seine Schelmenfüße
Und zischelt seine Grüße
In die verblüffte Welt.

Gehüllt in Niedertracht
Gleichwie in einer Wolke,

THE CHARACTER ASSASSINS

A breed of vermin lies
In dust and dry rot hidden,
As flame oft glows unbidden
In ashes and not dies.
Comes playful wind or rain
And wakes this baleful scourge,
From chaos swift emerge
Foul plague and fire and pain.

On booty bent there came
From his nocturnal cave
A pocket-picking knave.
But he finds better game:
He finds a flag torn down,
The facts of knowledge muddled,
A people all befuddled
By discord's petty frown.

On all sides he finds slums,
Depression's aimlessness,
And now in shamelessness
A prophet he becomes;
His blessings are unfurled,
As he bestrides destruction
To hiss his foul instruction
To the bedeviled world.

All clothed in scoundrelcy
As in a turgid cloud,

Ein Lügner vor dem Volke,
Ragt bald er groß an Macht
Mit seiner Helfer Zahl,
Die, hoch und niedrig stehend,
Gelegenheit erspähend,
Sich bieten seiner Wahl.

Sie teilen aus sein Wort,
Wie einst die Gottesboten
Getan mit den fünf Broten,
Das klecket fort und fort!
Erst log allein der Hund,
Nun lügen ihrer tausend;
Und wie ein Sturm erbrausend,
So wuchert jetzt sein Pfund.

Hoch schießt empor die Saat,
Verwandelt sind die Lande,
Die Menge lebt in Schande
Und lacht der Schofeltat!
Jetzt hat sich auch erwahrt,
Was erstlich war erfunden:
Die Guten sind verschwunden,
Die Schlechten stehn geschart!

Wenn einstmals diese Not
Lang wie ein Eis gebrochen,
Dann wird davon gesprochen,
Wie von dem schwarzen Tod;
Und einen Strohmann baun
Die Kinder auf der Heide,
Zu brennen Lust aus Leide
Und Licht aus altem Graun.

A public liar loud,
A mighty pow'r is he
With helpers manifold
In high and lowly station,
Each seeking elevation,
And each to his will sold.

His gospel word they spread,
It multiplies apace,
As once God's men of grace
Dealt out five loaves of bread.
The dog first lies alone,
Then thousands tell his lies;
His dim wit magnifies
Into a storm full blown.

A mighty harvest breeds,
The lands are ne'er the same,
The masses live in shame
And laugh at knavish deeds!
And now it has come true,
The warning no one feared:
The good have disappeared,
The bad are in full view.

When someday hence this ague
Like ice at length is broken,
We'll speak of it in token
As of bubonic plague.
And children will of straw
Make effigies on the plain,
New joy to burn from pain
And light from ancient awe.

Harold Lenz

SIEHST DU DEN STERN

Siehst du den Stern im fernsten Blau,
Der flimmernd fast erbleicht?
Sein Licht braucht eine Ewigkeit,
Bis es dein Aug erreicht!

Vielleicht vor tausend Jahren schon
Zu Asche stob der Stern;
Und doch steht dort sein milder Schein
Noch immer still und fern.

Dem Wesen solchen Scheines gleicht,
Der ist und doch nicht ist,
O Lieb, dein anmutvolles Sein,
Wenn du gestorben bist!

SEE THERE THE STAR

See there the star. In distant blue
Its twinkle almost dies.
Its light took an eternity
Until it reached your eyes.

A thousand years ago perhaps
In ashes fell that star,
And yet, up there its gentle light
Keeps shining still and far.

Quite like that star, quite like its light
Which shines because it shone,
O love, I sense thy cherished warmth
Since thou art dead and gone.

Alexander Gode

ABENDLIED

Augen, meine lieben Fensterlein,
Gebt mir schon so lange holden Schein,
Lasset freundlich Bild um Bild herein:
Einmal werdet ihr verdunkelt sein!

Fallen einst die müden Lider zu,
Löscht ihr aus, dann hat die Seele Ruh;
Tastend streift sie ab die Wanderschuh,
Legt sich auch in ihre finstre Truh.

Noch zwei Fünklein sieht sie glimmend stehn,
Wie zwei Sternlein, innerlich zu sehn,
Bis sie schwanken, und dann auch vergehn,
Wie von eines Falters Flügelwehn.

Doch noch wandl ich auf dem Abendfeld,
Nur dem sinkenden Gestirn gesellt;
Trinkt, o Augen, was die Wimper hält,
Von dem goldnen Überfluß der Welt.

EVENING SONG

Eyes, ye treasured windows of my sight,
Have so long allowed me precious light;
Letting hosts of images delight,
Ere the fall of nature's darkening night.

When some day your weary lids must close,
Light fades out, the soul can find repose;
Gropingly her shoes aside she throws,
Lays her in her coffin so morose.

Yet two sparks she sees aglow on high,
Like two stars that charm the inner eye,
Till they flicker, and they too must die,
Wafted off on wings of butterfly.

Still I linger on the evening weald,
With the sinking sun to share the field,
Drink, O eyes, all that the lashes shield
Of the golden wealth the world doth yield.

D. G. Wright

Conrad Ferdinand Meyer

DER RÖMISCHE BRUNNEN

Aufsteigt der Strahl und fallend gießt
Er voll der Marmorschale Rund,
Die, sich verschleiernd, überfließt
In einer zweiten Schale Grund;
Die zweite gibt, sie wird zu reich,
Der dritten wallend ihre Flut,
Und jede nimmt und gibt zugleich
Und strömt und ruht.

THE ROMAN FOUNTAIN

Up shoots the stream and falling pours
Its flood into the marble urn,
Which, veiled in lacey froth, outpours
Into a lower bowl in turn;
To still a third its surplus store
The second gives and rolling grows;
Each gives and takes forevermore
And rests and flows. . .

Isabel S. MacInnes

FÜLLE

Genug ist nicht genug! Gepriesen werde
Der Herbst! Kein Ast, der seiner Frucht entbehrte!
Tief beugt sich mancher allzureich beschwerte,
Der Apfel fällt mit dumpfem Laut zur Erde.

Genug ist nicht genug! Es lacht im Laube!
Die saftige Pfirsche winkt dem durstigen Munde!
Die trunknen Wespen summen in die Runde:
„Genug ist nicht genug!" um eine Traube.

Genug ist nicht genug! Mit vollen Zügen
Schlürft Dichtergeist am Borne des Genusses,
Das Herz, auch es bedarf des Überflusses,
Genug kann nie und nimmermehr genügen!

ABUNDANCE

Enough is not enough! Glory to Autumn!
No bough but bears its harvest, ripe and sound.
Some, overladen, bend beneath their burden.
An apple softly thuds upon the ground.

Enough is not enough! Laughter in copses.
The juicy peach beckons the thirsty tongue.
And drunken wasps cluster around the grapevine —
"Enough is not enough!" their buzzing song.

Enough is not enough! From all this plenty
Drink greedy gulps of joy to fire the brain.
The heart, too, needs its surfeit of abundance.
Enough can never be enough again.

Helen Sebba

ZWEI SEGEL

Zwei Segel erhellend
Die tiefblaue Bucht!
Zwei Segel sich schwellend
Zu ruhiger Flucht!

Wie eins in den Winden
Sich wölbt und bewegt,
Wird auch das Empfinden
Des andern erregt.

Begehrt eins zu hasten,
Das andre geht schnell,
Verlangt eins zu rasten,
Ruht auch sein Gesell.

TWO SAILS

Two sails make bright
The dark-blue bay;
Two sails stretch tight
To heave away.

When wind pours through,
One grows immense;
The other one, too,
Responds and is tense.

When one makes a run
Locked is their gait;
When calm strikes the one,
The other will wait.

Kurt J. Fickert

DER GESANG DES MEERES

Wolken, meine Kinder, wandern gehen
Wollt ihr? Fahret wohl! Auf Wiedersehen!
Eure wandellustigen Gestalten
Kann ich nicht in Mutterbanden halten.

Ihr langweilet euch auf meinen Wogen,
Dort die Erde hat euch angezogen:
Küsten, Klippen und des Leuchtturms Feuer!
Ziehet, Kinder! Geht auf Abenteuer!

Segelt, kühne Schiffer, in den Lüften!
Such die Gipfel! Ruhet über Klüften!
Brauet Stürme! Blitzet! Liefert Schlachten!
Traget glüh'nden Kampfes Purpurtrachten!

Rauscht im Regen! Murmelt in den Quellen!
Füllt die Brunnen! Rieselt in die Wellen!
Braust in Strömen durch die Lande nieder –
Kommet, meine Kinder, kommet wieder!

THE SONG OF THE SEA

Oh clouds, my children, is your will to roam?
Then go! Farewell, until you come back home!
I can no more your restless shapes retain
Within the bonds of my maternal rein

Now you are weary of my waves, I see,
The land has lured you there away from me:
The shores, the cliffs, the beacon's fiery glow!
Be off, and seek adventure, children, go!

Float, fearless sailors, gently through the air!
Seek hill-tops, and ravines, and linger there!
Engender storms, and strike with blinding light!
And don the purple garb of ardent fight!

Rush in the rain! Murmur in springs below!
Refresh the wells! Ripple in ebb and flow!
Stream down in torrents gushing through the plain,
And come, my children, back to me again!

D. G. Wright

JETZT REDE DU

Du warest mir ein täglich Wanderziel,
Viellieber Wald, in dumpfen Jugendtagen,
Ich hatte dir geträumten Glücks so viel
Anzuvertraun, so wahren Schmerz zu klagen.

Und wieder such ich dich, du dunkler Hort,
Und deines Wipfelmeers gewaltig Rauschen –
Jetzt rede du! Ich lasse dir das Wort!
Verstummt ist Klag und Jubel. Ich will lauschen.

NOW YOU SHALL SPEAK

Once you were daily pilgrimage to me,
Beloved wood, when I was young and sad,
And told you all my dreams of happiness
And all the real troubles that I had.

Now once again I seek your dim retreat
Where winds, like tides in treetops, rush and darken.
Now you shall speak! I leave the words to you!
Stilled are my joys and troubles. I shall hearken.

Frances Stillman

NACH EINEM NIEDERLÄNDER

Der Meister malt ein kleines, zartes Bild,
Zurückgelehnt beschaut ers liebevoll.
Es pocht. „Herein." Ein flämischer Junker ists
Mit einer drallen, aufgedonnerten Dirn,
Der vor Gesundheit fast die Wange birst.
Sie rauscht von Seide, flimmert von Geschmeid.
„Wir habens eilig, lieber Meister. Wißt,
Ein wackrer Schelm stiehlt mir das Töchterlein.
Morgen ist Hochzeit. Malet mir mein Kind!"
„Zur Stunde, Herr! Nur noch den Pinselstrich!"
Sie treten lustig vor die Staffelei:
Auf einem blanken Kissen schlummernd liegt
Ein feiner Mädchenkopf. Der Meister setzt
Des Blumenkranzes tiefste Knospe noch
Auf die verblichne Stirn mit leichter Hand.
– „Nach der Natur?" – „Nach der Natur. Mein Kind.
Gestern beerdigt. Herr, ich bin zu Dienst."

AFTER A DUTCH MASTER

The master paints a portrait, small but fine.
He stands aside and looks at it with love.
A knock. "Come in!" A Flemish baron leads
His daughter in: a coarse and gaudy wench
Whose rosy cheeks betoken perfect health.
Her silk gown rustles; her jewels flash light.
"Our time is precious, honored sir.
A lusty rogue intends to steal my girl from me.
Tomorrow they'll be wed. So paint my child!"
"At once, my Lord. Permit this final stroke."
With merry laugh they step before the easel.
Upon a cushion smooth, a lovely girl
Has laid her head. She sleeps. The master paints
With skillful hand the final flowret still,
Upon the leafy garland round the pale
And faded brow. "From life?" the baron asks.
"From life. My child. I buried her but
Yesterday . . . My lord, my time is yours."

Daniel Coogan

CHOR DER TOTEN

Wir Toten, wir Toten sind größere Heere
Als ihr auf der Erde, als ihr auf dem Meere!
Wir pflügten das Feld mit geduldigen Taten,
Ihr schwinget die Sichel und schneidet die Saaten,
Und was wir vollendet und was wir begonnen,
Das füllt noch dort oben die rauschenden Bronnen,
Und all unser Lieben und Hassen und Hadern,
Das klopft noch dort oben in sterblichen Adern,
Und was wir an gültigen Sätzen gefunden,
Dran bleibt aller irdische Wandel gebunden,
Und unsere Töne, Gebilde, Gedichte
Erkämpfen den Lorbeer im strahlenden Lichte,
Wir suchen noch immer die menschlichen Ziele –
Drum ehret und opfert! Denn unser sind viele!

THE CHORUS OF THE DEAD

We dead men, we dead men can muster more legions
Than all of you mortals in all the world's regions!
Where we ploughed the fields for the deeds we were sowing
There now sinks the harvest your sickles are mowing,
And what we completed or merely decided
Up there keeps your fountains with water provided,
And all our loving and hating and yearning,
Up there warms your blood and you still feel it burning,
By laws and by measures which we once erected
Still all that you do in your world is directed,
And what we in stone, sound, or word once created
Is crowned in the light by the world it elated.
We still are pursuing the goals of the living.
Revere our numbers. We still are the giving.

                                        Meno Spann

AM HIMMELSTOR

Mir träumt, ich komm ans Himmelstor
Und finde dich, die Süße!
Du saßest bei dem Quell davor
Und wuschest dir die Füße.

Du wuschest, wuschest ohne Rast
Den blendend weißen Schimmer,
Begannst mit wunderlicher Hast
Dein Werk von neuem immer.

Ich frug: ,,Was badest du dich hier
Mit tränennassen Wangen?''
Du sprachst: ,,Weil ich im Staub mit dir,
So tief im Staub gegangen.''

AT THE GATE OF HEAVEN

I dreamt I came to heaven's gate,
And found you there, my sweet!
Beside the fountain you did wait,
And bathe your dainty feet.

You washed the shimmer dazzling white,
You washed with might and main,
Then hastily, a curious sight,
Began all o'er again.

I asked: What makes you bathe your feet?
Your eyes, what makes them weep?"
"I walked," you said, "with you a street
On which the dust lay deep."

D. G. Wright

Heinrich Leuthold

BLÄTTERFALL

Leise, windverwehte Lieder,
Mögt ihr fallen in den Sand!
Blätter seid ihr eines Baumes,
Welcher nie in Blüte stand.

Welke, windverwehte Blätter,
Boten naher Winterruh,
Fallet sacht! . . . ihr deckt die Gräber
Mancher toten Hoffnung zu.

LEAF FALL

Soft melodies, wafted on winds,
Float down, on sands to rest!
You are the leaves of some fine tree,
With blossom never blessed.

Leaves, withered, and blown on the winds,
That winter's rest betide,
Fall gently! . . . for you clothe the graves
Of many hopes that died.

D. G. Wright

Robert Hamerling

DIE STERNE

Tausend goldne Sterne winken
Aus des Himmels blauer Höh';
Tausend goldne Sterne blinken
Aus dem spiegelglatten See.

Hoch hinan in blaue Ferne
Winken sie mit goldnem Licht;
Aufwärts, aufwärts zög' ich gerne,
Doch mein Flug erreicht sie nicht.

Nach der Erde hin, der feuchten,
Lockt mich ihr demantner Kranz;
Aber ach, die dort mir leuchten,
Sind ein wesenloser Glanz.

Und so mögt ihr, goldne Sterne,
Unsres Glücks Symbole sein:
Was der Himmel ist, ist ferne,
Was die Erde hat, ist Schein.

THE STARS

Golden stars in thousands shimmer
From the heaven's far beyond;
Golden stars in thousands glimmer,
From the smooth, unrippled pond.

High away in distant azure,
Twinkling with their golden light;
Upwards would I soar with pleasure,
Still they'd lie beyond my flight.

Down to this damp earth again, their
Diamond crowns alluring seem;
Those that brightly shine for me there
Hold such insubstantial gleam.

Golden stars may be portentous
Symbols of our destiny:
What heaven is, is far beyond us,
What earth has, is vanity.

D. G. Wright

Wilhelm Busch

DER KÜHNE RITTER UND DER GREULICHE LINDWURM

Es kroch der alte Drache
Aus seinem Felsgemache
Mit grausigem Randal.
All Jahr' ein Mägdlein wollt' er.
Sonst grollt' er und radollt' er,
Fraß alles ratzekahl.

Was kommt da aus dem Tore
In schwarzem Trauerflore
Für eine Prozession?
Die Königstochter Irme
Bringt man dem Lindenwurme;
Das Scheusal wartet schon.

Hurra! Wohl aus dem Holze
Ein Ritter keck und stolze
Sprengt her wie Wettersturm.
Er sticht dem Untier schnelle
Durch seine harte Pelle;
Tot liegt und schlapp der Wurm.

Da sprach der König freudig:
,,Wohlan, Herr Ritter schneidig,
Setzt euch bei uns zur Ruh.
Ich geb euch sporenstreiches
Die Hälfte meines Reiches,
Mein Töchterlein dazu!''

THE BOLD KNIGHT AND THE GRUESOME DRAGON

There came from rocky dwelling
The ancient dragon swelling
With fearful roaring sound.
Yearly a maid he wanted,
Or dire revenge he vaunted,
Ate everything he found.

What's from the gateway nearing,
In mourning black appearing?
Procession it must be.
For Irma, royal daughter,
Is being led to slaughter,
The gruesome victim she.

Hurrah! A knight comes storming,
Like tempest that is forming,
All proudly held his head.
The monster quickly struck he,
His lance through hard skin stuck he;
The dragon limp lies dead.

Then spoke the king delighted:
"Bold knight, when you've alighted
Come, sit with us and rest.
For straightway I am giving
You half of all my living,
And daughter, fair and best."

„Mau, Mau!" so rief erschrocken
Mit aufgesträubten Locken
Der Ritter stolz und keck.
„Ich hatte schon mal eine,
Die sitzt mir noch im Beine;
Ade!" und ritt ums Eck.

Mein kleinster Fehler ist der Neid. –
Aufrichtigkeit, Bescheidenheit,
Dienstfertigkeit und Frömmigkeit,
Obschon es herrlich schöne Gaben,
Die gönn' ich allen, die sie haben.
Nur, wenn ich sehe, daß der Schlechte
Das kriegt, was ich gern selber möchte;
Nur wenn ich leider in der Nähe
So viele böse Menschen sehe,
Und wenn ich dann so oft bemerke,
Wie sie durch sittenlose Werke
Den lasterhaften Leib ergötzen,
Das freilich tut mich tief verletzen.
Sonst, wie gesagt, bin ich hienieden
Gottlobunddank so recht zufrieden.

"No! No! there's been an error!"
His wild locks showed his terror,
The bold, brave knight did say.
"I've had a wife already,
She's had me good and steady!
Goodbye!" and rode away.

Francis Owen

My smallest fault is jealousy –
Honesty and modesty,
Obligingness and piety,
All fine traits, I here confess them,
No grudge 'gainst those who may possess them,
But when I see the villain grabbing
What I myself had planned on having;
And when I see right here around me
Enough of evil to astound me,
And when I see these people taking,
Unchaste desires ever waking,
Delight in all this sinful pleasure,
That hurts me deeply, without measure –
Otherwise, as I above have hinted,
I'm here below, thank heaven, contented.

Francis Owen

Wenn mir mal ein Malheur passiert,
Ich weiß, so bist du sehr gerührt.
Du denkst, es wäre doch fatal,
Passierte dir das auch einmal.
Doch weil das böse Schmerzensding
Zum Glück an dir vorüberging,
So ist die Sache anderseits
Für dich nicht ohne allen Reiz.
Du merkst, daß die Bedauerei
So eine Art von Wonne sei.

When a misfortune happens me,
I know you're sorry as can be.
You think it would be very bad,
If such misfortune you had had.
But since the evil came not nigh,
And fortunately passed you by,
And I was victim of the harm,
It's not for you without all charm.
You notice that commiseration
May be a kind of exaltation.

Francis Owen

LEIDER!

So ist's in alter Zeit gewesen,
So ist es, fürcht ich, auch noch heut.
Wer nicht besonders auserlesen,
Dem macht die Tugend Schwierigkeit.

Aufsteigend mußt Du Dich bemühen,
Doch ohne Mühe sinkest Du.
Der liebe Gott muß immer ziehen,
Dem Teufel fällt's von selber zu.

TOO BAD!

It was this way in times gone past,
It is this way and it will be,
He, who is not of chosen caste
Has problems with morality.

The path uphill is weariful;
But painless is the downward drift.
The Lord must pull and pull and pull,
To Satan fall you as a gift.

Dagmar Lange

Ferdinand von Saar

AUF EINEN ALTEN SCHLOSSPARK

Nie hat die Lust als Ariadnefaden
Sich durch dies grüne Labyrinth gezogen;
Man glättete hier stets des Lebens Wogen
Zum Teich Bethesda, um sich rein zu baden.

Eremitagen, Grotten an den Pfaden
Für schöne Seelen, die sich selbst belogen,
Als sie sich nannten von der Welt betrogen,
Und brünstig sah'n nach himmlischen Gestaden.

Hier stand die Zeit still, die, vom blut'gen Ruhme
Des Korsen kaum befreit, demütig wieder
Zu Füßen sank dem alten Heiligtume.

Hier weh'n noch Matthissons schwermüt'ge Lieder,
Hier blüht und duftet noch die blaue Blume,
Und wandelt Stillings Geist noch auf und nieder.

ON AN OLD CASTLE-PARK

Desire has never, through this maze's green,
Charted its way like Ariadne's thread;
Here life's waves were always smoothed and led
Into Bethesda's pond, to bathe men clean.

Grottoes and arbors lined this serpentine
For lofty spirits, who each time they said
The world had tricked them, tricked themselves instead,
Dreaming in pious lust of heaven's demesne.

Here time, which from Napoleon's bloody fame
Had scarcely been set free, stood still to pay
Its humble homage at the old god's flame.

Here hang the notes of Matthisson's sad lay,
Here the blue flower's perfume clings the same,
And here the ghost of Stilling goes its way.

George C. Schoolfield

Martin Greif

VOR DER ERNTE

Nun störet die Ähren im Felde
Ein leiser Hauch,
Wenn eine sich beugt, so bebet
Die andre auch.

Es ist, als ahnten sie alle
Der Sichel Schnitt –
Die Blumen und fremden Halme
Erzittern mit.

BEFORE THE HARVEST

Now all of the grain stalks stir
To a whispered breeze;
When two of them tremble, the others
Tremble with these.

They seem to be sensing the ruin
The scythe will strew;
The flowers and grainless grasses
Are trembling too.

Clark Stillman

Christian Wagner

SYRINGEN

Fast überirdisch dünkt mich euer Grüßen,
Syringen ihr, mit eurem Duft, dem süßen!

Wohl darf ich euch nach Geisterweise werten:
Ein schwellend Duftlied seid ihr von Verklärten.

Gott, wie ich doch in dieser blauen Kühle
Der Blumenwolke hier mich wohlig fühle!

Süß heimlich ahnend, was hineinverwoben,
Wie fühl ich mich so frei, so stolz gehoben!

Bin ich es selbst, des einstig Erdenwesen
Nun auch einmal zu solchem Glanz genesen?

Sinds meine Lieben, die, ach, längst begraben,
In diesen Düften Fühlung mit mir haben?

LILACS

As if from heaven so you now me greet
You lilac blossoms with your scent so sweet.

In spirit-like demeanor I evoke you best:
A swelling, fragrant song of souls at rest.

God, how since coming to this coolness blue
Of blooming cloud, I tranquil, happy grew.

In secret, sweetly sensing how 't was spun,
I feel exalted, lifted to the sun.

Is it myself who once to earth was bound
And now in splendor his reward has found?

Are they my loved ones who, long in their graves,
Communicate with me through fragrant waves?

Dorothea M. Singer

Friedrich Nietzsche

DAS TRUNKENE LIED

O Mensch! Gib acht!
Was spricht die tiefe Mitternacht?
,,Ich schlief, ich schlief –,
Aus tiefem Traum bin ich erwacht: –
Die Welt ist tief,
Und tiefer als der Tag gedacht.
Tief ist ihr Weh –,
Lust – tiefer noch als Herzeleid:
Weh spricht: Vergeh!
Doch alle Lust will Ewigkeit –,
Will tiefe, tiefe Ewigkeit!"

SONG OF RAPTURE

Oh men, give heed!
What is deep Midnight saying?
"I have been sleeping, sleeping –
And wake now from the dream where I was straying: –
This world below
Is deeper far than Day can guess.
Deep is its woe –
Joy – deeper than heart's pain can go:
'Begone!' Woe says,
But every Joy wants everlastingness –
Wants deeper, deeper everlastingness!"

Frances Stillman

Detlev von Liliencron

DIE MUSIK KOMMT

Klingling, bumbum und tschingdada,
Zieht im Triumph der Perserschah?
Und um die Ecke brausend brichts
Wie Tubaton des Weltgerichts,
Voran der Schellenträger.

Brumbrum, das große Bombardon,
Der Beckenschlag, das Helikon,
Die Pikkolo, der Zinkenist,
Die Türkentrommel, der Flötist,
Und dann der Herre Hauptmann.

Der Hauptmann naht mit stolzem Sinn,
Die Schuppenketten unterm Kinn,
Die Schärpe schnürt den schlanken Leib,
Beim Zeus! das ist kein Zeitvertreib;
Und dann die Herren Leutnants.

Zwei Leutnants, rosenrot und braun,
Die Fahne schützen sie als Zaun,
Die Fahne kommt, den Hut nimm ab,
Der bleiben treu wir bis ins Grab!
Und dann die Grenadiere.

Der Grenadier im strammen Tritt,
In Schritt und Tritt und Tritt und Schritt,
Das stampft und dröhnt und klappt und flirrt,
Laternenglas und Fenster klirrt;
Und dann die kleinen Mädchen.

THE BAND MARCHES

Klingling, boomboom, and chingdada –
A triumph of the Persian Shah?
It rounds the corner with a boom
Like trumpets of the Day of Doom,
In front the big drum major.

Broombroom, the monster bombardon,
The cymbals and the helicon,
The cornet and the piccolo,
The big bass drum, the flute also,
And then the lord high captain.

The haughty captain comes in sight.
His helmet strap is neat and tight;
A tight sash gives a martial air –
By Jove, this is no light affair!
And then the fine lieutenants.

The two lieutenants, red and tan,
Surround the flag, a wall of man!
The flag arrives: take off your hat –
We will be true till death to that!
And then the common privates.

The privates march with martial step,
With hep! and step, and step and hep!
They stamp and rumble, clatter, shake,
Till window panes and streetlights quake –
And then the little schoolgirls.

Die Mädchen alle, Kopf an Kopf,
Das Auge blau und blond der Zopf,
Aus Tür und Tor und Hof und Haus
Schaut Mine, Trine, Stine aus;
Vorbei ist die Musike.

Klingling, tschingtsching und Paukenkrach,
Noch aus der Ferne tönt es schwach,
Ganz leise bumbum bumbum tsching;
Zog da ein bunter Schmetterling,
Tschingtsching, bum, um die Ecke?

The little girls, head after head —
From door and gate and yard and shed,
With eyes of blue and pigtailed hair,
How Betty, Hetty, Letty stare.
The music has departed.

Klingling, chingching, and kettledrums,
Faint from the distance still it comes,
Quite softly, boomboomboomboom ching —
Did a bright butterfly take wing,
Chingching, boom, round the corner?

Calvin S. Brown

INDEX OF
TITLES AND BEGINNINGS OF GERMAN POEMS

INDEX OF TRANSLATORS